The Senders

The Senders

WORLD MISSIONS CONFERENCES
AND
FAITH PROMISE OFFERINGS

Paul B. Smith

G.R. WELCH COMPANY, LIMITED
Toronto   Canada

By the same author: *Church Aflame*
After Midnight
Naked Truth
World Conquest
Headline Pulpit
Perilous Times
Other Gospels
Daily Gospel
Eastward to Moscow
The Question of South Africa
The Church on the Brink

Scripture quotations used in *The Senders: World Missions Conferences and Faith Promise Offerings* are from the King James' Version of *The Holy Bible*.

ISBN: 0-919532-53-5

G.R. Welch Company, Limited
Toronto, M8Z 1J9, Canada

© 1979 by G.R. Welch Company, Limited

All rights reserved. No part of this publication may be reproduced, stored in a retrieval system, or transmitted in any form or by any means without prior permission of the copyright owner.

Printed in Canada

Contents

Step Out in Faith   vi
Foreword I   ix
Foreword II   xi
Foreword III   xiii
Preface   1
1 Give Your Conference Priority   5
2 One Way to Organize It   9
    About Speakers   9
    About National Christian Leaders   13
    About Missionaries   15
    About New Recruits   16
    About Pictures   16
    About Music   17
    About the Program   18
    The Exhibit Room   21
    The Mottoes   22
    The Food Service   24
    The Youth Banquet   25
    The Fellowship Breakfast   26
    The Conference Leadership   28
    The Briefing   30
3 When You Brief Your Guests   33
    Be Positive and Optimistic   33
    Be Realistic   33
    Nationals and Missionaries   37
    Personal Appeals   39
    Special Emphasis   41
4 The Importance of a Missionary Policy   43
    Missionary Policy of The Peoples Church   44
5 A Word About Words   49
6 Don't Be Afraid of Money   53
7 The Principles of Christian Giving   57
8 The Faith Promise   67
9 The Same Thing Another Way   79
10 A "Five-Year Plan"   83
11 Let's Admit the Bottleneck   89
12 Christian Priorities   93
13 We Will Now Receive the Offering   97
14 How Can We Hear God Speak?   105
15 God's Four Calls   115

I am destined to proclaim the message,
  unmindful of personal consequences to myself.

Zinzendorf

Foreword I

My heart was thrilled as I studied this book. I read every word of it. My — what tremendous experiences! Thinking of the beginning of the work, I could only cry out, "What hath God wrought!"

It is not often that only two men, a father and a son, could be the sole leaders and pastors of a church for a period of well over fifty years. What an amazing miracle of God's grace!

This great work started in Massey Hall on September 9, 1928. I was the pastor until December 31, 1958. My son, Paul, became the senior minister on January 1, 1959. He has told of instance after instance that he has seen with his own eyes ever since he took charge, and the end is not yet.

During the time I held the pastorate, many letters came to my desk asking me to explain the large missionary offerings. However, I was too busy getting our program launched to give any thought to books about it. But now, my son has done what I could not do.

I am not going to repeat what he has written except to say that I endorse every word of it and pray that it may be a great and rich blessing to all who read it. Since Paul has been in charge, the Sunday School has increased to 1800 and a day school has been founded and is in operation with nearly 700 students. The missionary offering has risen from about $300,000 to $1,500,000 each year. And after all, it is just a working and professional man's church.

Souls are saved at almost every evangelistic service. The women's prayer meeting still goes on. The number of elders has grown from about a hundred to nearly three hundred. The choir and orchestra have remained strong until they now fill all of the available platform space, which is huge. The great building into which we sometimes packed two thousand has been replaced by a new auditorium on Sheppard Avenue, where we can pack in nearly three thousand.

Dr. Paul has written well and this book on missionary conferences will be read with breathless interest. May all those rejoice who see the work of world missions expanding — very often as a result of conferences like these.

However, I am not going to deal with the methods here. I leave the book itself to do that. It is the church that prospers at home that God will use to reach men for Jesus Christ in foreign lands. *The Senders* could be used as a textbook on missions in every Bible school and conference in the nation.

God has given me a wise and gifted son, and every church needs such a pastor if it is to succeed. Put missions first and God will do the rest. If you cannot be a missionary abroad then be one at home, and the blessing will be yours, for you serve the God of the impossible. He wants to use you in a way that you never dreamed possible. If The Peoples Church can see thirteen million dollars raised for world missions, why cannot others do the same?

Dr. Oswald J. Smith
The Peoples Church
Toronto, Ontario July 1979

Foreword II

We are living in a day when many voices are telling us we have seriously failed to carry out the Great Commission. Dr. Ralph Winter and many others tell us of the two billion, four hundred million people alive today who have never heard enough of the gospel to make a decision for salvation. Moreover these great blocks of lost people have no contiguous evangelical church to reach them.

Yet at the same time we are receiving reports of unprecedented response to the gospel especially in Africa, Latin America and in some Asian countries. Even while scores of new churches are being started every day, and some denominations, as in Korea, are increasing by better than sixty percent a year, these other 2,400,000,000 haven't heard.

We also must face the fact that many of the old line denominations in Canada, the U.S.A. and Europe who once were the great mission-sending churches, are today retrenching to an alarming degree. Bible-believing, missionary-sending churches are greatly increasing their efforts but have done little more than make up the losses of missionary staff from the older groups.

Interestingly enough it isn't just missionaries that are needed but the greater problem is, or will be, financial support to send out missionaries from both the developed and developing nations.

This is the thesis of the author of this book on how to hold a missions conference. Dr. Paul B. Smith has been involved in missionary conferences all of his life. Few people have had the opportunity that he has had to see such conferences in action as well as visit active missions all over the world. For over fifty years, first under the direction of his father Dr. Oswald J. Smith, and now under his own leadership, The Peoples Church of Toronto has held missions conferences. It is known worldwide for its support and interest in world missions.

Dr. Smith is sure that the only method for getting sufficient money to finance this greatest of all world enterprises is to involve millions of Christians in evangelical churches in mission conferences. He tells how such conferences can give the necessary missions education, inspiration, and challenge to provide the missionaries and the money to reach the world for Christ. He also proves that a missions-centered church never has problems supporting the local church program.

Out of his rich experience he tells the reader how to do it. The Peoples Church has proved that it can be done. Its hundreds of missionary volunteers and its more than a million dollar faith promise offering each year are sufficient credentials. From my personal participation in several hundred such conferences, I am confident that this volume can be a valuable handbook for any pastor whose heart is burdened for world missions and who wants to see his church join with thousands of others in making world missions possible.

>   Dr. Clyde W. Taylor
>   Arnold, Maryland, September 1979

Foreword III

Few men would be as qualified to write a book about missionary conferences in local churches as Dr. Paul Smith. Perhaps no one would be *better* qualified than he. Paul Smith grew up in the atmosphere of annual missionary conferences in the renowned Peoples Church of Toronto. And since becoming the senior pastor of that church he has admirably organized and conducted these conferences in a continuing and successful way. He has also been called to many other churches — in many countries — to lead or participate in similar conferences. The known record speaks for itself.

This book is unique in several ways. First, the subject itself is fairly unique. Who else has written a complete book about mission conventions? Also, the many details of such a convention which are dealt with here are extremely impressive and informative. Then too, the frankness and boldness with which Dr. Smith has written are very pointed. The author deals candidly with how to keep all speakers and participants in a missionary conference in line and in harmony with the nature and objective of the entire conference program — no small task. Someone needed to address this point and Smith has done it, factually and frankly.

The book focuses on the missionary program used in The Peoples Church where it has proved so fruitful over the years. Dr. Paul has introduced certain changes in recent conventions, and it may be that more changes will seem feasible with the passing of time. Admittedly, as the author himself concedes in the development of his thesis, not all the details of the plan spelled out here will fit every local situation, but I am convinced that the general pattern is both biblical and practical and that if followed in any normal church will prove spiritually productive.

One thing that comes through strongly in this unusual book is that the missionary conference in the local church must be given high priority in the church's annual program, and that the pastor — or senior pastor in the case of large congregation — shall be its promoter and conductor. The entire staff must be involved in carrying out the many necessary details related to the convention, but the pastor is to be the chief and visible figure.

I have counted my personal friendship with Dr. Paul Smith a

true privilege and I am extremely pleased that he has produced this book. To say I am happy to write this foreword is to understate the fact. I sincerely commend this treatise to concerned Christians in churches everywhere, particularly to pastors and readers. Read it. Reread it. Study it. Put it into practice. God will bless.

Dr. G. Christian Weiss
Bella Vista, Arkansas, September 1979

Preface

"How-to" books can easily become egotistical and carnal.

Egotistical, because they usually sound as if the author is bragging, "I know how to do it, and nobody else does." Or, "If you don't do it my way, it won't work." God forbid that this little book on missionary conferences and faith promise offerings should turn out like that.

On the other hand, every author should be aware of the fact that he has some credentials that give him the authority to write. In most cases the human authors of the Bible took time to give their credentials — particularly the apostle Paul. Perhaps because he considered himself to be the "chief" of sinners and "the least of the apostles" he knew that people would pay no attention to his writings unless they knew that his credentials were valid.

I met an author once who never gave his name to his work. He told me that humility demanded that he must not associate himself with his books. I felt that he was being dishonest to the public by not signing his name. Readers have a right to know who wrote a book or an article. It is important that we know not only what has been said, but also, who said it. Anonymous books are like anonymous letters — not worth wasting time over.

My association with world missions began when I was born. I attended my first missionary conference as soon as I could walk. I made my first "faith promise" offering when I was eight years old.

I was born in 1921 when my father pastored the Christian and Missionary Alliance Church in Toronto, Canada. I attended The Peoples Church the day it was opened and I have been in every missionary conference that has ever been held there — more than fifty.

I have also had the privilege of being one of the main speakers at scores of conferences in other churches all over the world. I don't have the complete list, but since I began to keep records, I have been a speaker at more than one hundred and forty-two missionary conventions that have included a great variety of denominations. Fifty-four of these have been in Presbyterian churches and thirty-six in Baptist churches. In addition to more than a dozen other denominational groups, my missionary conference ministry has included five colleges and universities, ten Bible conferences, nine foreign countries outside of North America and a few fund-raising banquets.

My assignment at these conventions has been to speak about missions and usually to emphasize the financial aspect so that the pastor can take some sort of offering. In some cases I have been expected to actually go ahead and ask for the offering — usually, a faith promise offering, but I prefer to have the local pastor or chairman do this.

In the course of these conferences I have had the honor of working with missionaries, nationals and other missions speakers from all over the world — almost every country and colony. From these extremely knowledgeable people I have been able to learn a great deal about almost every conceivable aspect of world missions. I owe them a debt that I can never repay, but I am able to pass their knowledge and know-how on to thousands of others.

The three people who have helped me most would have to be my own father, Dr. Oswald J. Smith; Dr. Clyde W. Taylor, and Dr. G. Christian Weiss.

I guess my father's genius has been his simplicity — his ability to eliminate the irrelevant and the confusing, and to see the main points. All my basic principles about missions are the result of the fact that I happened to be born in his house and couldn't help but absorb some of his missionary knowledge and zeal to get the job done.

Clyde Taylor has been my human encyclopedia on missions and he has been gracious enough over many years to teach me a little of the vast amount he knows. I doubt if he is even aware of the fact that this has happened, but I have been fortunate in crossing paths with him in many places and hearing him often in the conventions in my church. I am grateful for what he has done to help missionaries in our generation and for what he has done to help me.

I met G. Christian Weiss when he was the general director of the Gospel Missionary Union during the early years of my ministry. I like to think that he has the same sort of mind as I, in the respect that he wants to see everything laid out in a very logical form and usually tied to an unforgettable outline. He was a missionary in Morocco before I met him and I spent some time with him in conferences during the time he was trying to get clearance from the Lord about whether or not he should accept Dr. Theodore Epp's invitation to become the missionary voice of the Back to the Bible Broadcast. Since then we have been colleagues in many missionary conferences and he has taught me a great deal.

Many others have had an influence on my life, and thus on this book, but these three will always predominate.

Teaching is invaluable but never as practical as when it can be hitched to the wheels of experience and made into some kind of effective vehicle. My practical training started with my first trip overseas in 1946. Since then I have taken twenty-six world trips and visited seventy-one countries. This has enabled me to see just about all kinds of missionary work both in modernistic cultures such as Europe and Japan and among primitive peoples such as the Xhosa, Zulu and Basuto tribes in the reserves of South Africa and the stone-age Dani tribe of Irian Jaya.

I've lived in five-star hotels in densely populated cities in India and in small homes in the mountains of Korea. In 1958 I wrote home and described our Korean house: "...about thirty feet long and eight or ten feet wide. The length is divided into three parts. The center is the kitchen and the two end sections are our rooms. The kitchen is sunk into the earth several feet and there are passages leading under the floors of the other two rooms through which the heat from the kitchen fire penetrates. This means that there is a sort of radiant heating in the floors of these rooms. The floor is made out of mud and is covered with ordinary brown paper. When the mud hardens you have a perfectly smooth brown paper floor — radiant heated. We sleep in sleeping bags." I've also lived in big hotels in Korea and primitive huts in India.

The fortune of my birth, the patience of my teachers and the experience of my travels have given me some grasp of the task of world evangelization and some familiarity with the methods that may accomplish it. My involvement in evangelism for thirteen years and then the same pastorate for twenty-seven years has made me aware of the problems that confront the sending churches and the means by which they may fulfill their commission to reach the world.

This kind of book may appear carnal because it concentrates on *our* efforts rather than God's power. However, it is quite unscriptural to expect God to do everything. The intrinsic structure of the Great Commission incorporates a union of our efforts and God's power. This is the way our Lord planned it. He does not do it all. He expects us to help. We are commanded to go.

He has promised to be with us. We are urged to preach and witness. He has assured us that He will produce the results. When Jesus fed the five thousand He ordered the disciples to organize them into small groups that could be managed. When He planned the last supper, the disciples went ahead to make the necessary arrangements. When the apostle Paul took the first faith promise offering he organized it in detail months ahead of time.

It was Paul who reminded his converts that they were co-laborers with Christ. It is true that some of the things we do are not spiritual — not spiritual in the sense that they involve many physical activities like advertising, promotion, set-up, office work, traveling, and so on. But these carnal activities are clothed in spirituality when we do them in absolute dependence upon God — knowing that they are never an end in themselves and are only valid when God infuses the power that causes the miracle.

This book is intended to be egotistical and carnal in the proper scriptural context of those concepts. It is my heart-cry that my little practical suggestions may be like the boy's lunch — blessed by Jesus and multiplied to you.

Paul B. Smith

1

Give Your Conference Priority

World evangelization should not be treated as a minor endeavor, but as the major enterprise of the church.

Most Christians associate the word "missions" with things that are unimportant, inferior, or uninteresting. We think of little groups of ladies drinking afternoon tea and cutting up bandages; church basements cluttered with an array of clothing; household articles that are no longer useful in this country being sold at ridiculous prices; colored slides of far away places — many of which cannot be seen because of poor photography or inadequate projection equipment, or moving pictures that produce more headaches than heartaches because very often they have been taken by rank amateurs from the backs of elephants or fast-moving trains. We may think of people whom we conclude have gone to the foreign field because they were not capable of doing anything better at home.

Maybe that's why some very fine people won't even use the word missions anymore — that is, in its old-fashioned plural form. They prefer to talk of "mission," singular. I can understand this, but I think the argument is purely a case of semantics and I don't think it matters which form the word takes as long as we know what we mean when we use it. In either case the word may have a plural or singular connotation. The expression "world mission" may sometimes refer to the singleness of the task or it may be used in a sort of collective sense that brings to mind the plurality of the task. I believe the same is true of "world missions." Generally, I think of this expression as a single task, and so I follow it with a singular verb. On other occasions it brings before my mind a collection of things, and then I connect it with a plural verb. In these pages, when I use the word I will stick to the older expression and hope that my "world mission" friends will understand what I am attempting to say.

At any rate, these odd things that I have listed do not represent true missions, but unfortunately have become associated with missions. It is little wonder that in the average church, missions has been relegated to one small department of the work.

In The Peoples Church, to avoid these unjust accusations of real missionary work, we choose to use the expression "world evangelization," and the moment it passes our lips we think of concentrated effort; sacrificial giving; vivid pictorial presentation of the greatest battle ever fought; well-trained men and women who could make an adequate mark for themselves in the homeland, and a united campaign in which every department and organization of the church has joined. This is true only because world evangelization has been put in its proper place — not a minor department but the major enterprise.

Every year we have a conference on world evangelization: call it a Missionary Convention, a World Vision Crusade, or World Missions Conference, as you wish. During this period we concentrate on missions to the exclusion of everything else that we may be doing. Most churches do this for every other department of their work, but not for missions. Time may be set aside for evangelistic crusades; a week blocked out for the annual Bible conference; special speakers brought in to conduct a prophetic series, and Daily Vacation Bible School held for the children. But there is no concerted effort to promote world evangelization.

An occasional missionary Sunday, an isolated missionary offering, or a few missionary speakers throughout the year, will never make the people of any church realize that the task of world evangelization is of vital importance. There must be a time when everything else stops, and all the machinery of the church is converted and used on the missionary production line.

The Time

The World Missions Conference should be scheduled during the best time of the year. If we hold it when the snow is falling or the farmers are working or the people are on their vacations, we are admitting that it is not really important. We have relegated it to a season that is not good for any other kinds of meetings. Choose the best time of the year for the people of your church so that there will be no valid reason why they cannot attend it regularly.

The length of time will differ depending on the church and the working habits of the people around it. Sometimes the conference can be concentrated into a weekend that starts on Friday night and finishes on Sunday night. In other places it may be more suitable to begin with the usual midweek service on Wednesday night and go through Sunday night. A great many churches hold their conference for a full eight days — that is Sunday through Sunday. In The Peoples Church, Toronto, there were some years a long time ago when our conference lasted for four weeks and five Sundays! However, during the last fifteen years we have learned that maintaining any sort of consistent attendance for that long a period is quite impractical in our city and now we run it for two full weeks, including three Sundays.

Usually the terminal point of a missionary conference will be some kind of offering — perhaps a "faith promise" offering. It should be remembered that in any church it is almost impossible to get a complete commitment of the adherents on any one Sunday. That is why it is valuable to extend the offering over at least two Sundays so that you can get the maximum participation of your people. Even if the conference itself is shorter than this, you will find that it is valuable to take the faith promise offering once again on the Sunday immediately following the conference. This is the only way that you can be sure that a maximum number of your adherents will have an opportunity of participating.

Counter-attractions

It is vitally important that no other official activity be carried on in the church during the missionary conference. There should be no other meetings of any kind. Practices should be eliminated completely or at least reduced to the bare necessity. Class executive meetings can be held during some other week. Of course, no organization of the church should even dream of holding any sort of social activity during the one period of the year when the rest of the church is concentrating upon meeting the needs of dying people.

Let the whole church put world evangelization where it belongs. It is not a by-product but *the* product. It is not a department but the united effort of the entire organization. It is not a preliminary bout but the main event. It is not a sideshow but the feature attraction. It is not a lane in the country but the main street of the city. It is not a pilot boat but the battleship. It is not a skirmish but the main thrust of the battle. *World evangelization should not be treated as a minor endeavor but as the major enterprise of the church.*

2

One Way to Organize It

There are many ways a World Missions Conference can be organized. I am going to mention the things that we have found successful in the work of The Peoples Church. However, it should be remembered that this is only one of many methods. I have attended conferences all over the country where different things have been done and the general nature of the conference is quite different from ours but nevertheless the results have been effective. The methods we use in our church in Toronto have worked for more than fifty years and have produced what may be the largest income for world missions in the world — apart from some of the large denominational churches that contribute to a general fund where much of the money is spent on many things that are not really missionary in nature.

About Speakers

Every session of the convention should feature one outstanding missionary speaker. He may be a missionary, a pastor who has led his people in a great missionary program, or a gifted deputational worker. When we choose a speaker in The Peoples Church, we must have a man who has been gifted by God to communicate with a large crowd. His presentation must be attractive to the people and he must have a strong voice so that they can hear what he has to say.

There are many excellent missionaries who are very poor public speakers. It is possible for a missionary to be invaluable on the foreign field but a poor deputational worker in the homeland, and sometimes the most outstanding deputational worker does not make the best missionary. There are a few remarkable people who seem to have both gifts. Their major task on the field may not be one that demands much communication but when necessary during their furlough, they may be excellent speakers. However, this is a rare combination and not often found in one person.

Almost everywhere I go the pastor asks me to recommend

speakers for his church's World Missions Conference. Even verbally I hesitate to do this because I am aware of the fact that everyone is not effective in every place. There are some people who might be able to communicate with my congregation in a magnificent manner but in your situation they might be quite ineffective. However, this book would not be complete without giving churches at least some idea of the kinds of people who would be suitable for the main speaking post in a World Missions Conference.

I am going to list these people, knowing that I will be leaving out some of the most important speakers of this nature in the world today. Please remember that this is not a list of recommended speakers but rather a list of people indicative of the kind of person who has been used effectively in the missionary conferences of The Peoples Church. As far as I know now, the people I list are still alive but even if they have gone to be with their Lord, the list will still give you some concept of the type of person about whom we are talking.

When thinking about speakers for a World Missions Conference you should remember that there is a great deal of difference between a good Bible teacher and a good missions speaker. There are some people who are able to do both but remember that you are having a conference in order to saturate the people of your church with information, inspiration and exhortation about world missions. Therefore, your main speaker should be the kind of person who can zero in on this subject in particular and, of course, give the biblical basis for it.

There are some conferences where, for one reason or another, there is at least one service per day that is of a Bible teaching nature. I can understand this and where it is feasible it can be an asset to the conference, but whatever you do, remember that the Bible teacher should never take the place of the missionary speaker. They are not the same kind of person and they do not bring the same kinds of results with their ministry. I have been in some churches that combined missions, Bible teaching and evangelism all within the same week and they did a magnificent job of it. However, we are concerned for the most part in these pages with the church that wants to put on a World Missions Conference that will highlight the cause of missions as that cause is highlighted at no other time of the year.

Here are a few of the people whom we have used in the World

Missions Conferences of The Peoples Church over a period of a great many years. Again let me say this list is by no means exhaustive — and it represents only people who have been in our church. There are a great many others whom we have not had the privilege of including in our roster of speakers to this date, but perhaps this will act as a guideline to pastors and committees who are wondering about the problem of main speakers:

Brother Andrew, God's Smuggler, Open Doors, Orange, California
Charles E. Blair, Pastor, Calvary Temple, Denver, Colorado
George M. Cowan, President, Wycliffe Bible Translators
Peter Deyneka, Founder, Slavic Gospel Association, Chicago
Peter Deyneka, Jr., General Director, Slavic Gospel Association, Chicago
Paul E. Finkenbinder, President, Hermano Pablo, Inc., Costa Rica
Allen Finley, Christian Nationals' Evangelism Commission, San Jose, California
Edward S. Graffam, Director of World Relief Commission of the National Association of Evangelicals (retired)
Garth W. Hunt, Living Bibles International, Vancouver, B.C.
Dick Hillis, Founder, Overseas Crusades
Don Hillis, Director, Evangelical Alliance Mission
Paul E. Kauffman, Founder & Director, Asian Outreach, Hong Kong
Edwin W. Kilbourne, Vice President at Large, OMS International
Jack McAlister, President, World Literature Crusade, California
George C. Middleton, Founder, Emmanuel Relief & Rehabilitation
Kenneth E. Moon, Pastor, Northside Baptist Church, St. Petersburg, Florida
John Harold Ockenga, President, Gordon Conwell Seminary, Boston, Massachusetts (retired)
Kenn W. Opperman, Leadership Development International, Inc., Atlanta, Georgia
Peter Stamm, Director, Africa Inland Mission
Clyde W. Taylor, Founder of Evangelical Foreign Missions Association (retired)

J. Allen Thompson, President, World Team, Coral Ridge, Florida
Paul Toms, Minister, Park Street Church, Boston, Massachusetts
William C. Townsend, Founder, Wycliffe Bible Translators
G. Christian Weiss, Back to the Bible Broadcast, Lincoln, Nebraska (retired)
Jim Wilson, Youth for Christ International
Ravi Zacharias, International Evangelist, Toronto

This is a dangerous list to even attempt, not only because I have undoubtedly left out some who have been very important to our own conferences and many others who are being used constantly in other conferences, but also because by now some of these speakers may be dead, have changed positions, retired, or perhaps even left the ministry. Addresses are not exact, but I think I have identified each sufficiently to be traced. In some cases the names may serve to remind you of others with similar gifts.

In addition to these I should mention four of my own associates who have been exposed to our conferences for years.

The Rev. B. Keith Whiticar has worked very closely with me at the organizational level of our conferences. He may know more of the logistical details than I do and he is an excellent preacher and gifted in leading workshops.

Dr. Daniel L. Edmundson has been my associate over a period of nearly fifteen years. His particular field is Christian education, but he is a fine preacher, a deeply spiritual person and extremely knowledgeable when it comes to missions. He has had a great deal of experience in The Peoples Church and has been the main speaker at many other conferences.

Dr. George C. Billings takes charge of The Peoples Church whenever I am away and is quite capable of handling the work if I were to retire. He was reared in the church, but has had extensive experience as a pastor in main-line denominational churches both in Canada and the United States. He had spent more than eleven years in a Southern Baptist Church just before he accepted our call to his home church in the capacity of senior associate minister. He is a brilliant speaker and highly cognizant of a worldwide missionary work.

Dr. David E. Williams knows more about the musical part of a missionary conference than any other quartet of musical ministers put together. He is not a preacher, but for those who have questions about this part of the program, Dr. Williams knows a lot of the answers.

In platform personnel you will have a great deal of choice if you remember that world missions is common ground for just about all evangelicals. Presbyterians should feel free to invite Baptists. Calvinists can work together with Armenians. Charismatics and non-Charismatics don't have to argue over missions. This is one area where God's people can contribute to each other and at the same time maintain their own distinctives.

In our Toronto church we insist that our speaking and singing guests are evangelicals, fundamentalists in the original sense of the term, true to the Scriptures and accepting no other authority but the Bible, with a good reputation both at home and abroad and associated with a church or a board that can be identified as completely reliable. These people will be ladies and gentlemen and when they are with you they will stick to "missions" and not dream of offending anyone by emphasizing some minor doctrine they know your church does not accept.

There are many others. Some have preached in our conferences in Toronto, some haven't. There are a few "nationals" who would be effective main speakers, but most of them are limited to some extent by a language barrier and in other cases, even though they may speak our language fluently, their accent may be difficult for our people to follow.

Sometimes the general director of a mission is a good speaker, but not always. Usually, such a person needs to be more of an administrator than a communicator. There are some missionaries who could be added to this list, but remember that these are only suggestions as to the kind of person who can fill the role of your main speaker.

About National Christian Leaders

During the past ten years most of us have been alerted to the fact that the face of World Missions has changed dramatically. One of the major changes has been that some of the national leaders and their churches have taken over the predominant positions on the mission fields in their own countries, and in most cases today foreign missionaries work at the request of leaders of national churches and, for the most part, under their direction.

For this reason we generally bring a number of national Christian leaders to each of our conferences and give them a few minutes at each service to present the work in their countries. It is generally better to have several nationals so that your people get a good view of a variety of countries rather than limiting them to one. In most cases you will find that the nationals will do better if their time is limited. I usually give them a maximum of fifteen minutes and then grade this down to as low as three minutes. On some occasions I introduce the nationals in the form of an interview. This can be good as it adds variety to the program.

Some of the nationals are not extremely fluent in your language and it may be a little difficult for the people to understand them if they give a long address. Of course, there are some remarkable exceptions to this. Remember that most of the nationals are able to speak several languages including English whereas most of us do well if we can communicate in English alone.

I always urge my national speakers to give due credit to the work of the foreign missionaries without whom in most cases there would have been no national churches whatsoever. Generally they are very glad to do this and recognize the debt they owe the foreign missionary. As a matter of fact most nationals will be quick to recognize the work of the foreign missionaries without any prompting at all. However, in any kind of church programming whether it's nationals, foreign missionaries, keynote speakers or musicians, it is important to tell your guests what you expect from them. They will do far better if they know, and most of them are there to help your church. If they are not cooperative, there is no need to fuss with them. Just be careful that you do not invite them to return.

I also insist that none of the speakers make special appeals for funds to support any of their personal projects. We reserve the right as a church to make decisions about where and how the money of our people will be spent and we do not want to have them influenced by the passionate appeal that is often made by a good public communicator unless we have decided officially to back his project and have asked him to make this kind of an appeal.

All of these things will take a bit of ruthlessness on your part. Some of your guests will object — particularly to their time limitation, but you should be supported by two things in this connection: First, tell them not to waste their limited time by complaining about it. Whatever time they are given starts from the time they get up to speak — not after they have objected to their time limit. Second, remember that you are planning your conference for the best possible results in *your* country and culture — not in Korea, Latin America or some other place where the culture may in fact allow for more time than you have. Don't let your guests embarrass you into doing things — such as prolonging a service — that you know won't work in your town. Be ruthless at this point.

About Missionaries

It is difficult to conduct a World Missions Conference without missionaries. The more missionaries there are in a convention, the more missionary atmosphere there will be. Missionaries who are home on furlough should be invited to the conference so that they can be kept before the people and mingle with them. Apart from any platform work they may do, we have found that the personal contact of missionaries with the adherents of The Peoples Church has been invaluable. In recent years we have had nearly one hundred and fifty missionaries at our conferences, but most of them have not spoken on the main platform at all. We have them minister in our Sunday School classes, but to a large extent the speaking of national leaders in our conferences has taken the place of that of the missionaries.

When you do not have any nationals, of course, it is a good thing to have the missionaries speak as a part of the main program, but once again their time should be limited so that there can be a variety of fields presented. Often you will find ways to present both nationals and missionaries. Nationals have some advantage just because they are from another country.

Both missionaries and nationals should be urged not to preach sermons or expound scripture, but rather to tell the people about the work on their fields of service. I always ask them to be positive and optimistic rather than negative and pessimistic. It is true that there are many problems in the world that make world missions difficult, but during the course of a conference the objective is to encourage people to give their time, in some cases their lives, and in most cases their money and prayer as a dedication to God for the evangelization of the world. Your people do not want to support a losing cause. We need to emphasize the fact that God knows exactly what He is doing and is right on time.

About New Recruits

Most conferences have found that one of the greatest sources of stimulation toward missionary giving is the presence and testimonies of new recruits or candidates for the foreign mission fields of the world. Almost every society will have such people who have already been trained and are prepared to go. These folk should be presented *very briefly* to the people at almost every service. You will discover that the new recruits are not only an incentive to missionary giving but will prove to be a tremendous source of inspiration for missionary volunteering on the part of the people of your church. Yet in The Peoples Church we seldom present new recruits publicly simply in the interest of time. It is important to limit the service to a length of time that is comfortable for the people of your area. This means that you will have to be selective in what is presented and what is eliminated.

A few missionaries, recruits and nationals feel that it is a waste of their time to stay at a conference where they don't speak very much from the main platform. Nothing could be farther from the truth. Churches need these people in their conferences to add their spiritual power, their person-to-person contact with the people and their flesh-and-blood demonstration that they are just ordinary human beings who have dedicated their lives to God for a very specialized type of service. It is great if these folk get a chance to communicate verbally, but they should never feel slighted because their speaking time is held to a minimum.

About Pictures

Pictures give the people an opportunity to see the work as well as hear about it. We have used at least three different kinds of pictorial presentations: sound motion pictures with a dramatic missionary story; sound motion pictures with a documentary commentary; and 35 mm colored slides.

Christian film companies and the missionary societies themselves have produced many fine dramatic films on world evangelization. These are usually most interesting, and sometimes instructive. The documentary-type film does not attract a large crowd but has more of an educational value. Increasing rapidly in popularity are the 35 mm colored slides, with which a good speaker can tell a much more complete story than can be presented through any motion film with a sound track. Nowadays technology has enabled missionary societies to prepare a commentary that runs on a sound track with the slides and thus, if necessary, they can be presented without the missionary who produced them actually being present. Some societies have produced elaborate multi-media pictorial presentations which can be extremely valuable.

Once again in the interest of time you should choose short pictorial presentations. The sound motion picture films should never be more than thirty minutes in length and it is much more preferable if they run between fifteen and twenty minutes. Fifteen or twenty minutes should also be adequate for any other kind of picture presentation — that is unless you wish the pictures to take the place of the main message. On some occasions you will find that this is a valid thing to do.

The chief type of pictures to guard against are those that have no spiritual message, and those which foist poor photography upon captive congregations. It is just as useless to show pictures which cannot be seen properly as it is to present a speaker who cannot be heard. Thanks to some good training and much improved equipment for the amateur photographer, missionary pictures have improved tremendously. As a matter of fact, it has been a few years since I have seen any really bad pictures. The best rule I ever learned about photography is to have enough courage to throw away the poor pictures: take many; stay in the sunshine, and be ruthless about not using the bad ones.

About Music

Most churches would not hold an evangelistic campaign without bringing a special speaker and some sort of musicians. We are just as careful to plan a good spiritual musical program during missionary week as we are for any other special effort. It is not necessary for all of the music to be strictly of a missionary nature as long as the congregation concentrates on the great missionary hymns. Special numbers can be chosen from any of the gospel songs that will add inspiration to the services.

When I speak of special music, I mean outside groups or soloists that are "professional" in the best Christian sense of the term. Even though some of your local talent may be just as good or in some cases better than a visiting group or soloist, they will never draw as large a crowd because usually the people have heard them before and the World Missions Conference demands music that is interesting and *new* in its presentation. Outside means out of your general area completely. A group from some other local church is still local.

In any given service during our conference in Toronto we give our musicians two spots in which we ask them to take approximately six or seven minutes. This generally allows them to present two numbers in each spot. We always urge the musicians to limit their talking and concentrate upon their music. It can be devastating if the musicians decide to give long testimonies or explanations about their songs. Remember that in a conference of this nature you already have a number of speakers and the musicians are there for an entirely different sort of a presentation. Remind them of the fact that this is not a musical concert or even a normal Sunday night service. They are there to sing not to speak.

It is important that congregational singing should concentrate upon the missionary hymns and songs. There are a great many of them, and most regular hymnbooks will have a good variety. Do not take the people's minds off world missions by having them sing songs that you would normally sing at a Sunday morning worship service or during an evangelistic crusade.

You can gain a great deal of missionary mileage and education as far as your people are concerned through the magnificent words that have been set to music, those that bring a missionary message of some nature.

About the Program

In The Peoples Church we limit the main speaker to twenty-five minutes in every service. The nationals and/or missionaries combined are given approximately twenty minutes. In recent years we have not used pictures of any kind during the regular services. The only reason for this is that in the early days we used them a great deal and our people had become accustomed to them. It is important to remember that when any method wears out there is no purpose in staying with it.

In a World Missions Conference one of the secrets of success is change. There are many fine procedures that will last for a few years but then should be dropped and replaced by other methods. Unfortunately in much of our church work we seem to have adopted the thinking that what has always been done should be done in the future and for that reason we very often use methods that have long since been outdated, or if not outdated, our people have become so accustomed to them that they do not have as much effect.

A typical weeknight program in The Peoples Church conference might be as follows:

- Theme (usually presented by the choir, but not absolutely necessary)
- Opening Hymn (never more than three verses)
- Invocation (a prayer that should not last more than one minute)
- First musical package (approximately six minutes)
- The national and missionary speakers (approximately twenty minutes)
- Missionary Hymn (perhaps only two verses)
- Second musical package (approximately six or seven minutes)
- Main Speaker (approximately twenty-five minutes)
- Missionary Hymn (two verses)
- Announcements (the program for tomorrow — given while people are still standing)
- Announcement about the retiring offering

This is the *present* format of our program in the World Missions Conference. It is only a suggestion and by the time you read these pages we may have changed it drastically, but at the present time it works and works well.

It has been our custom to introduce speakers and musicians only once — that is the first time they appear. After that we simply let them get up and speak. This will save you a great deal of time in which very often you say nice things about your guest and then your guest feels that he must take time to say nice things about you and your church.

Also to save time we have eliminated asking for an offering during the service. In recent years we have received a retiring offering. We give the congregation an envelope for this purpose as they arrive. It is printed in a way that welcomes them to the service, explains that the speakers and singers may not be introduced and therefore lists them with a brief description in the order in which they will appear. There is a note to the effect that the envelope may be used for their retiring offering. I generally have this taken for some special project which may have been brought out in the course of the service itself. You will discover that people will give a great deal more for some missionary project than they will to the general expenses of the conference. In my opinion the expenses of the conference should be a part of the total missionary budget.

The order of service I have given is for those meetings during the week when a "faith promise" offering is not taken. When we receive a faith promise offering in our church — this usually happens at every Sunday service — the time of the speakers needs to be limited even further. Often, I take the offering after the nationals and missionaries have spoken. Then the main speaker can take a longer time — depending upon when your service should end — after the offering. If I have someone who can speak directly to the subject of giving (and these are very few and very far between) I put him on for fifteen minutes — not longer — before the offering and I receive the offering immediately after he finishes.

A message leading into an offering should be short. Time should be left to take the offering slowly, methodically and without apology. The pastor himself should learn how to do this. He should allow at least fifteen minutes for it, but not more than twenty.

Again let me emphasize the fact that any one method of conducting a World Missions Conference or of putting together the program for a given service will not work in every church. You should always adapt these methods to your own particular church and its denominational culture as well as your own community and the demands it may make upon your people.

In our situation in Toronto — and in most places where I have been in the United States — the total time for the average service in a missionary conference is approximately one hour and a half. There are very few places where it has to be less than this and in North America there are very few areas where it can be longer. Sometimes I have to remind my guests — both missionaries and nationals — from other countries that our culture is not the same as theirs and the fact that we may not be able to have a three-or four-hour service usually has nothing whatever to do with the spirituality of our people but rather it is connected with the kind of civilization in which we happen to live. Very often our dear friends from overseas will make unfortunate comparisons of the spirituality of our respective groups based on their ability to endure a long service, which really is not a scriptural basis.

The Exhibit Room

One of the basic purposes of a World Missions Conference is to give the people of the church as complete a missionary education as possible. Going, praying and giving should be based not only upon the inspiration of the Holy Spirit and "the Divine urge" but also on some good solid information. This is what a missionary conference can do. That is why many churches set up an exhibit room. This is a place where the missionaries or missions are represented and display any curios from their fields that they may have, and make accessible to the people literature that describes what is going on in their areas of service. In many cases some sort of light refreshment is made available in the exhibit room and the missionaries, of course, should be there standing close to their exhibits so that they can engage the people in conversation.

For at least thirty-five years in The Peoples Church we had always had an exhibit room and it was one of the highlights of our conventions. However, when I first started conducting the World Missions Conferences some years ago I noticed that the exhibit room was used more for Christian fellowship than for gaining a missionary education. Some nights I would go into the exhibit room and find that the missionaries were standing alone by their exhibit booths while the people were having a great time together eating cookies and drinking tea and coffee, etc. Obviously the original purpose of the exhibit room in our situation had worn off and to the dismay of some of my older people we decided to do without it for a few years at least.

On the other hand, if your church has never had an exhibit room you will find it extremely fascinating and very informative to your people. The only thing that I would suggest is that you keep your eye on it carefully and if it seems to lose its validity as it did in our case, then you have obviously arrived at the time when it should be dropped or changed. Now, after more than ten years without our exhibit room we have revived it in The Peoples Church, and in its first year, 1979, it went great — but is subject to cancellation as soon as it may stop serving its purpose.

The Mottoes

Our main auditorium is decorated for the conference with the mottoes that have been used of God to inspire missionary endeavor. There are basically two kinds of mottoes: those that have been formulated by people, and those that are taken directly from the Scriptures. Here is a partial list that we have used, but undoubtedly there will be other mottoes with which you are familiar and we have not yet heard about. At any rate, mottoes can be very useful. They do a quiet sort of preaching while people are gathering, during the service, and as the people are leaving. Whatever you do, you should never be afraid of "mutilating" your sanctuary by putting up signs such as this as long as they serve a valid purpose. Remember that modern churches are not the Temple of God. They were never intended to be. Therefore the rules about the sacred nature of God's Temple do not apply to a church except insofar as Christian people who *are* the Temples of God are gathered in that particular building to worship.

Some of the mottoes we have used in The Peoples Church are:
You must go or send a substitute — Oswald J. Smith
Anywhere, provided it be forward — David Livingstone
If God wills the evangelization of the world, and you refuse to support missions, then you are opposed to the will of God — Oswald J. Smith
Attempt great things for God, expect great things from God — William Carey
A man may die leaving upwards of a million, without taking any of it upwards — William Fetler
Why should anyone hear the Gospel twice before everyone has heard it once? — Oswald J. Smith
If Jesus Christ be God and died for me, then no sacrifice can be too great for me to make for Him — C.T. Studd
Give according to your income lest God make your income according to your giving — Peter Marshall
The prospects are as bright as the promises of God — Adoniram Judson
Now let me burn out for Christ — Henry Martyn
Yet more, O my God, more toil, more agony, more suffering for Thee — Frances Xavier
The Church which ceases to be evangelistic will soon cease to be evangelical — Alexander Duff

Oh for a hundred thousand lives to be spent in the service of Christ — George Whitfield
You have one business on earth — to save souls — John Wesley
This generation can only reach this generation — Unknown
Only as the church fulfills her missionary obligation does she justify her existence — Unknown
The light that shines farthest shines brightest nearest home — Unknown
We can give without loving, but we cannot love without giving — Unknown
Not how much of my money will I give to God, but, how much of God's money will I keep for myself — Unknown
The supreme task of the Church is the evangelization of the world — Unknown

Mottoes we have taken from the Bible are:
The people that walked in darkness have seen a great light (Isa. 9:2).
Look unto me, and be ye saved, all the ends of the earth (Isa. 45:22).
At the name of Jesus every knee should bow (Phil. 2:10).
Lord, what wilt thou have me to do? (Acts 9:6),
Whom shall I send, and who will go for us? (Isa. 6:8).
Here am I; send me (Isa. 6:8).
We are ambassadors for Christ (2 Cor. 5:20).
Who will have all men to be saved (I Tim. 2:4).
Ye shall be witnesses unto me both in Jerusalem. . .and unto the uttermost part of the earth (Acts 1:8).
How shall they preach, except they be sent? (Rom. 10:15).
The isles shall wait for his law (Isa. 42:4).
My name shall be great among the heathen (Mal. 1:11).
Come over into Macedonia, and help us (Acts 16:9).
To every nation, and kindred, and tongue, and people (Rev. 14:6).
In thy seed shall all the nations of the earth be blessed (Gen. 22:18).
Declare his glory among the heathen (I Chron. 16:24).
Say among the heathen that the Lord reigneth (Psalm 96:10).
This gospel. . .shall be preached in all the world (Matt. 24:14).
Go ye therefore, and teach all nations (Matt. 28:19).
The gospel must first be published among all nations (Mark 13:10).

Go ye into all the world, and preach the gospel to every creature (Mark 16:15).
Repentance. . .should be preached in his name among all nations (Luke 24:47).
For a great door. . .is opened unto me (I Cor. 16:9).

One year we felt led to build our conference around the idea of time — and in particular, its brevity. The main theme was "Time is Running Out," but then we supported this with short quotations from the Bible bearing on time. Here are a few from which we had to choose:
It is time to seek the Lord! (Hos. 10:12)
It is high time to awake out of sleep! (Rom. 13:11)
Put ye in the sickle for the harvest is ripe (Joel 3:13)
He that sleepeth in harvest. . .causeth shame! (Prov. 10:5)
Come before winter! (II Tim. 4:21)
Redeeming the time! (Eph. 5:16)
The night is far spent! (Rom. 13:12)
The time is short! (I Cor. 7:29)
The night cometh! (John 9:4)
The time is come for thee to reap! (Rev. 14:15)

The Food Service

Perhaps it should be remembered that the early churches usually met in homes. This meant that there were kitchens, and undoubtedly food service was involved in the fellowship of these assemblies of God's people. It has been my experience that in the World Missions Conferences both here in Toronto and in scores of other places where I have had the privilege of ministering, a highlight of each conference was the fellowship that was made possible around the table — between the Christian people of the local church and the missionaries, nationals and other special guests.

In our conference in Toronto we have only four noon-hour meetings during the last week. This, again, has to do with our local situation in a large city in which daytime meetings are almost impossible to conduct — with any hope of a worthwhile attendance. For this reason we limit the daytime meetings to Tuesday, Wednesday, Thursday and Friday of the final week of our two-week conference. At the close of these noon-hour services we have a "soup and sandwich" buffet-style lunch that is made available to all of our conference personnel, local ministerial and secretarial staff and their guests — but not the public in general. This is only because we do not have adequate facilities to handle two or three hundred people at a noon-hour luncheon as our day school takes up all of these facilities at that time.

I have been in a number of churches where I have thoroughly enjoyed a regular luncheon that was served every weekday after a noon-hour service. In most cases this was open to the general public — that is, those who attended the service — and they proved to be an invaluable time of interaction in many different directions. In some cases a small charge was set to cover the cost and in other cases the cost was considered part of the total missionary involvement of the church.

The Youth Banquet

One of the most exciting and inspirational events we have in our conference is the Youth Interaction banquet. It is held on a Saturday night in the main ballroom of some hotel and is a "dress-up" dinner occasion.

Because of the high cost of such a meal in a nice place we usually subsidize it. The young people pay between half and two-thirds of the cost of the actual dinner. I raise the rest in the missionary offering — generally one of the retiring offerings. This is not at all difficult because most parents are eager to contribute to something that will help their own family and other young people.

Attendance is strictly limited to people thirty years of age and under — down to about thirteen or fourteen. Small children will ruin it for this age group! The only older guests are the missionaries, platform personnel and church staff, and we ask these folk to spread themselves as thin as possible. The idea is to have some such person at every table and we have found it best to use a room with round tables that seat eight or ten people.

The missionary is not at the table to preach, but to let the others see that missionaries are just regular people who are serving God full-time and usually in a foreign country. Sometimes they do this best by talking about a football game, the weather, waterskiing or anything else that people generally talk about. If this conversation turns naturally toward a discussion of missions, that's great. But if it doesn't, it's still great because for the first time some young people will have begun to associate World Missions with an evening of fun — maybe even the best night out in their year.

The program for this banquet should be geared for the kids — lots of music — maybe nearly all music, if you have a good group or soloist. Then there could be short testimonies by the nationals, preferably about aspects of their culture that are different from ours. Or the testimonies could be given by the missionaries. You could even have a twenty-minute message — if you have someone who knows how to communicate with young people. If there is a message it should not be evangelistic or Bible teaching, but missionary. The other subjects are heard throughout the whole year. This banquet is to promote missions.

In recent years we have received a "faith promise" offering at our youth banquet. The youth give toward the support of our own young people who are accepted by recognized boards to go on short-term missionary expeditions. These are designed by some of the major societies to let young people get involved in missionary work and at the same time see the mission field. The tours of duty are usually scheduled during the summer school break and limited to those who are in their final year of high school or are mature enough to be in college.

Many of our young people have completed one, and sometimes two, of these short-term ministries. The results have been excellent. In a few cases they come back fully intending to become missionaries. In others, they return to infuse a new spirit of missions among their peers that has sometimes resulted in more recruits, but always in more intelligent praying for and giving to the cause of missions.

In 1979 the youth banquet offering amounted to almost eighteen thousand dollars. This offering also enables us to send some of our youth musical groups to spend a short time on a mission field. In August of 1979 our "Set Free Singers" spent a week in the Republic of Haiti. They have never been the same since.

The Fellowship Breakfast

In 1975 we began to compensate for the Youth Interaction banquet by providing a special breakfast for our older people.

This is also held in one of the major hotels and usually draws a crowd of five or six hundred. We provide a full-course breakfast. In this case we insist the people be more than thirty years of age. However, the program differs in the respect that we have one of our main speakers, or sometimes even a special speaker brought in for that occasion only, give a thirty-minute address. Of course we also have our musical group sing one or two numbers at the breakfast.

As in the case of the youth banquet, we also charge something for the breakfast — perhaps two thirds of the total cost. Then we subsidize the balance from our World Missions budget. It has been our experience that unless people pay at least something for such an occasion they may forget to come or they may treat it rather lightly. Our point is to keep it as reasonable as possible in an extremely inflated society.

At the adult breakfast the offering is usually connected with some project that is presented by the main speaker. Such a project should be chosen very carefully and must be something that the church has been led to back officially. On several occasions it has been to provide Bibles for some of the nations that have never had any contemporary version of the Word of God, or perhaps no Bibles at all. One year it was for Living Bibles International. That offering came to forty thousand dollars. Another year it was for complete Bibles in the contemporary Mau script for Mainland China — thirty thousand dollars.

Sometimes it is a good thing to guard these offerings for special projects by setting a maximum amount that will be used for this purpose. Any balance can then go into the general missionary budget. If this is to be done, it should be made quite clear to the people when the offering is taken. In some cases these offerings have gone somewhat higher than our maximum goal. In others they have been less and we have made up the difference from general missionary funds.

One thing that will keep a missionary conference alive is a continual stream of new financial projects. Always maintain your basic commitments for the support of your missionaries or for any other program that is basic to the missionary vision of your church. But remember that people gradually lose interest in giving always to the same things.

One year we agreed to raise our share in the allowance of all our Canadian foreign workers. Another year we decided to assume the support of a number of national leaders. We added one hundred nationals in one year, and have maintained their support ever since. A number of years ago we received a specific offering for humanitarian relief work. This has continued and runs between one hundred and fifty and two hundred thousand dollars per year. This money is sent through the World Relief Commission of Canada and thus it is dispersed by evangelical workers and accompanied in most cases by some sort of gospel presentation. Our money has been designated over the years for the Southern Sahara disaster areas of Africa, and for Bangladesh, Guatemala and Haiti. The majority of these relief funds comes from our television audience.

Thus "food service" can be used to bring about fellowship, interaction with missionaries and nationals, and also contribute financially to your total missionary giving.

The Conference Leadership

The senior minister of the church should be the key man in the entire missionary endeavor as well as the conference. In an ideal situation it is better if he is chairman of the missionary committee and, of course, should be present at all their meetings, whether he is chairman or not. It is of paramount importance that the senior minister conducts all major services of the World Missions Conference.

Remember that the purpose of this kind of conference is to accentuate world missions and make this area of the work important in the eyes of your people. Perhaps the most obvious manner in which a church can say that some aspect of its ministry is of secondary importance is for the senior minister to absent himself from that department's affairs or to have no role in its activities. There are very few churches that would have an evangelistic crusade, a "revival meeting," a Bible conference, or almost any other major activity of the church unless the senior minister was the leader of all the services that these special efforts involved.

I have worked with some churches that have a fine missionary committee but it is quite obvious that the pastor of the church has left this entire area of work to these people. Although in his own mind he may feel that world missions is important, by separating himself from the activities of the committee he is indicating to the rest of the congregation that he really does not think missions is the supreme task of the church.

If the senior pastor does not cooperate in the missionary endeavor this does not mean that the missionary committee should stop its work as well. Sometimes the only endeavor to reach the world is carried on by the World Missions committee and without it there would be no missionary work whatsoever in some churches. I bow with great admiration and respect before the great missionary committees of churches across the world, but as a pastor I know that the majority of the congregation will never be completely sold on the *importance* of World Missions unless their senior pastor makes it obvious by being personally and completely involved. He will not leave the conduct of missions services and activities in the hands of other people.

Another reason for this is that the pastor is the only one who can really keep missions alive before the total congregation between conferences. Perhaps the question people ask more than any other involves this: "How do you maintain interest among your people between conferences?" The only answer that I know, that really works, is to have a pastor who is extremely missionary-minded. This means that very few major services will go by without some comment about the missionary program of the church. When the pastor is expounding any book of the Bible he will take whatever opportunity is available to emphasize the teaching of the entire Bible, particularly about the responsibility of the church to reach the world. Furthermore, from time to time he will remind his people of the missionary commitments of the church and the need to keep their faith promises up-to-date so that those commitments can be fulfilled.

Remember that in a faith promise offering we remind the people continually that nobody will go directly to them and ask for money. It is a relationship between the person and God. Sometimes we say that instructions for sending the money in will be sent through the mails, but apart from this we promise the people that we will not harrass them about payment. But this does not mean that we will not remind the people in general from the pulpit about their faith promise offerings and the church's commitment. The pastor is really the only one who is in a position to do this properly and thus keep the interest of the people alive between conferences.

The Briefing

Many years ago I attended a World Missions Conference in The First Presbyterian Church of Jackson, Mississippi where at that time Dr. John Reed Miller was the minister. I have returned to be a speaker at that conference for something like ten consecutive years. One of the things Dr. Miller taught me was to brief my platform personnel before every service. I remember he insisted that all of his guest speakers, missionaries and nationals gather with him in his office thirty minutes before the beginning of each service. At this meeting he would brief us on the program for that night and then have a short prayer with us.

Following in Dr. Miller's footsteps in this respect I have observed this policy for many years now in our World Missions Conferences. I insist that all our conference personnel gather with me for thirty minutes before the beginning of each service. This means that they must arrange their schedules in such a way that they can be at the church at least that much in advance of the meeting. At the briefing I do a number of things:

- I hand each of them a copy of the program for that service and go over it with them carefully so that each participant knows exactly when he is scheduled to appear and what we expect him to do.
- I talk about other plans we may have for succeeding days that will affect the schedules of the conference personnel. At this time I brief them about what is expected of them at the Fellowship Breakfast and the Youth Interaction Banquet and any other additional gatherings — such as Sunday School assignments — in which they may be involved. This gives them an opportunity not only of knowing what is happening but of having time to get adequately prepared in every way to fill a particular obligation.
- In almost every one of these briefing sessions I talk to the entire group about the time element in the services. There are a great many people who have the utmost difficulty in controlling the length of their talks or sermons and I explain to them that a World Missions Conference is not the results or the efforts of any one person or group. It is a "package" that in our situation involves two full weeks and a great many services and people. It is only insofar as each individual contributes to the total "package" that the

conference will be spiritually and materially successful.
- I also emphasize the fact that when one individual goes beyond his time he is literally robbing one of his colleagues of his time. When this is done with all of the group together it means that each person knows how long everyone else is supposed to minister. If one person should go beyond the allotted time period it is an infringement on the opportunities of others. There is nothing that can take the place of this sort of time pressure on your platform personnel, and telling them on one occasion is never enough. This principle must be reiterated many times throughout the conference — particularly in view of the fact that there will be new personnel arriving, in most cases, as the conference progresses.

I have dealt here with the kind of briefing that concerns each session. If you have an opportunity to give more time to your briefing at the beginning of the conference there are some other things of a more general nature that should be mentioned. The next chapter deals with some of these areas that I have stressed to all my guests in our initial briefing period.

3

When You Brief Your Guests

In a conference that lasts as long as ours it is usually possible to have a general briefing so that we can touch on a number of things that concern us in our guests' ministry. We choose the first occasion when most guests are with us. In our case this is usually the second Monday night. It is done after a hot dinner served at the church.

Be Positive and Optimistic

I ask all of our guests — speakers, missionaries, nationals and singers — to be positive and optimistic. We all know there are problems. Some of them are serious, but the place to discuss these is behind closed doors with small groups of people who are knowledgeable about missions. There is no place for pessimism and negativism on the main platform of a conference.

Don't cry over the closed doors. Rejoice over the open doors. Don't lament the mistakes of the past. Thank God that the future can be filled with success. Don't be sad about the missionary "casualties." Thank God for those who have stayed on the job for several terms or a lifetime.

No one is anxious to hitch his wagon to a falling star. People are eager to support something that is successful. Failure discourages folk and depressed congregations will have difficulty trying to get excited over a losing cause.

Be Realistic

I urge the foreign missionaries to be realistic. It is not necessary to depict themselves and their work as if they were a sort of modern David Livingstone.

I remember visiting the Republic of Haiti in 1949. It was my first experience on a mission field and my task was to speak for several days at the convention for the Haitian Christians connected with, what was at that time, the West Indies Mission.

I stayed in the home of one of the missionaries in a sort of compound. Actually it was a nice house with adequate facilities for those days — not a great deal different from the kind of accommodation most of us had then in Canada. Of course, it was built for the tropics and did not have a basement, heating system or insulation. My uncle, the Rev. Jack Depew, had rigged up a shower on the roof where the water was heated by the sun. The food was quite normal and we even had some Haitian folk who acted as maids. It was very comfortable.

After the convention the Rev. Kenneth Harold guided me on a trip back into the hills. It was very exciting and altogether different from anything I had ever seen before. After a day's ride on small Haitian horses through some rather treacherous hills and valleys we forded a river where the water reached well up to the horses' saddles. When we arrived at our destination...But let me quote the story directly from the pages of my diary:

April 2, 1949, 7:50 p.m.
The Interior of Haiti

I wish there was some way to give you an adequate picture of our activities this afternoon and this evening...We are now at our destination. We are sitting at this moment in the center room of a little three-roomed Haitian house. The walls are of white native plaster. The roof is thatched. The floor is simply dry mud, pressed hard and smooth with continual use. There is a plaid tablecloth on the table and a coal oil lamp in the center.

We have just finished a meal consisting of rice and beans, green bananas boiled, and yams — washed down with a glass of cold coconut water. It is now about seven-thirty. It is dark outside but dry.

In a few minutes we will probably string up our hammocks and retire.

April 3, 1949, 12:30 noon
In the same native hut

We did nothing all night; I did not even sleep. We did turn the flashlights on a few times to try and spot the rats that were running around on the rafters above us and now and then on our hammock ropes, but they seemed to know just about when the light was going to shine each time and managed somehow to get under cover before we saw them. I managed to get a fleeting glimpse of a tail disappearing into the thatch.

We awoke, or at least got up, at about six-thirty in the morning. After we had all washed in the same water we sat down to breakfast — coffee and sourdough bread. My trousers were still wet this morning when I pulled them on as a result of the dunking I received in the river last night. I spent the first hour of the day sitting out in the sunshine trying to get them dried out.

The ride back was very little different from the trip into the hills yesterday. At one point on the trail it became so steep that we had to get off our horses and lead them down an almost perpendicular drop. The horses skidded down on all fours and we jumped down.

In my diary this story went on and on, but this much will serve my purpose. The truth is that I spent most of my time in a very pleasant missionary compound at Aux Cayes, Haiti. I spent two days back in the hills beyond a place called Pico, but guess what my emphasis was when I returned to the United States and Canada? Of course, I talked about the convention at Aux Cayes, but the majority of the time I spent describing my trip into the hills. I'm sure I gave the impression that my short excursion to the thatched-roofed Haitian hut was typical of my missionary life in Haiti — difficult trails, treacherous rivers, repulsive rats and funny food.

It is true that most of the missionaries had made one or more of these expeditions, but this was not their normal life in Haiti. Even in 1949 they lived in comfortable homes on a pleasant compound with a group of friendly missionaries. They taught in the Bible school or worked at the clinic. Life was good and I had the impression that the last thing they wanted to do was to return home and live a monotonous life in much less happy conditions.

Still, as late as 1979 there persists the idea that all missionaries give up everything, live very primitively, guard themselves constantly from wild animals, are continually in grave danger, and of course, always eat funny food.

Most people think of missionaries as people who must preach. They are envisioned walking through jungle trails wearing white pith helmets and preaching to underprivileged and fearsome natives — generally having a different colored skin than the missionaries.

It would be my considered judgment that less than ten percent of the total missionary force either lives primitively or spends its time preaching. The few who live in primitive surroundings are usually Bible translators whose work demands living with the people. However, even these, though isolated from civilization, do not live the kind of life the very early pioneers endured. When I was in Irian Jaya in January of 1979 I stayed with missionaries of the Christian and Missionary Alliance and also in one of the stations of the Wycliffe Bible Translators.

In both cases they lived in small clearings in dense jungles surrounded by mountains sometimes rising as high as sixteen thousand feet. But they had nice houses in the jungle, excellent food and were in constant touch with headquarters by radio. If there had been an emergency, Missionary Aviation Fellowship or Jaars (Wycliffe's Jungle Aviation and Radio Service) aircraft could have reached them with help within a few hours.

Preaching is not the major task of the average modern missionary. Most of them do other things — run printing presses, fix machines, teach school, doctor or nurse people, operate radio controls, pound typewriters, run business machines, fix teeth, sell books in Christian bookshops, administer offices, construct buildings, run pharmacies, teach English — you name it, they do it. Most of the things ordinary people like us do here, they do there. A few workers are still pioneering new areas and do some preaching, but for the most part the preaching is done by the nationals. The missionary is an aide. Usually he goes to work for the nationals at the request of the national church. He may never preach, but be extremely effective in getting some job done.

I ask my missionary guests to be realistic about how they live and what they do. If they live in a highrise apartment in a big city, drive a car to an office every day and do the work of a business person, I want our people to know it. Raising support does not depend on painting a sacrificial picture of these things. Most Christians at home are eager to support people who know what they're doing and are doing it in the most modern and efficient way possible. They appreciate a missionary who has enough judgment to take care of himself physically and mentally by living as adequately as his field of service permits. I rejoice when I see people on the mission field who are living comfortably enough to get the very best out of their God-given ability.

Civilized or pioneer work appeals to different folk. At home many people enjoy "roughing it." Every weekend witness the campers who crowd our highways to get to wilderness areas. They can't wait to leave their push-button homes behind and get back to nature.

There are still some mission fields where this sort of life is necessary, but many of our Christians just do not appreciate thatched-roofed huts, dangerous animals and funny food. By far the majority of mission fields do not require any of these.

If someone wants to preach, there are a few foreign mission preaching points left — but not many. If one is not gifted in public speaking, the majority of fields do not need it.

I have a strong conviction that God generally allows us to do the things we like best and He uses the abilities we already have. When I was younger I sometimes got the impression that God was sort of mean. If a person had a real aversion to a certain country, that's exactly where God would force him to go. If a girl was frightened of animals, God would rather maliciously send her to a field that was overrun by the most ferocious beasts. If someone was adept at fixing machines but a poor public communicator, God would put him where there were no machines, but a lot of talking was necessary. . .and so on.

There may be an occasional case where God calls a person with a bad speech impediment and makes an evangelist out of him. But this is the exception — not the general rule. Most Christian workers are using their talents to do what they do best. They are living where they want to live and enjoying every moment of it.

This is what I mean when I ask the foreign missionaries to be realistic.

Nationals and Missionaries

I have talked about the roles of nationals and missionaries in our common task. In my general briefing I ask the missionaries to promote the nationals and say quite frankly how much all of us depend upon them and how impossible our work would be without them.

But I also ask the nationals to be careful they do not leave the impression that in our modern world we no longer need the foreign missionary. The cross-cultural missionary is always needed — in every country including the traditional Christian nations. Of course, in the few remaining primitive fields the work would never even get started without the missionary, but they are equally necessary in countries where some other religion is so aggressive and dominant that there have been only a few converts. Such countries simply do not have enough national Christians to do all that should be done.

In addition, there is a sense in which even where there is an active and large national constituency, the missionary is always a pioneer. He has a different perspective than the local person. He has had some advantages in his own country that enable him to see new areas of work and different methods that the national has never seen. As the missionary works himself out of any given job — which he should do, then he is free to divert his attention to tasks that no one else has seen or has had time for.

It was my great honor to speak at the convention of the Open Air Campaigners in 1954 in what was then called the Presbyterian Assembly Hall in the heart of Sydney, Australia. During my crusades in Australia I had been impressed by their unique methods of doing open air work in many places outside the normal churches. They worked on the streets, at the beaches, in the factories, at sporting events, and so on. But they had developed open air work into a very fine art. It was obvious that they had enjoyed a success in this area that we in North America had never achieved.

At that one meeting I urged some of them to come to North America and show us how to do it. I'm sure that other people and events had far more influence over their decision than my simple exhortation, but at any rate they came. Now for well over twenty years the Open Air Campaigners have been sending missionaries to Canada and the United States. They didn't come to evangelize us or build us up in the faith. They came to pioneer an area of work with which the nationals in our countries needed help.

In the same way Americans have sometimes gone to other Christian countries to pioneer the use of contemporary gospel music in a manner that those countries had never attempted before. These were American pioneer missionaries to places like Great Britain, Australia, New Zealand, etc.

There is no doubt that Koreans are well able to carry on their own work and support it, but there are many areas in which the foreign missionary not only helps the Korean church, but pioneers in departments that the nationals of that country have either not been aware of or have not had the time for. On the other hand it would be good for North America if some Korean missionaries came to us and spent some time as pioneers in the area of prayer. Certainly, Koreans seem to know more about prayer than most Americans or Canadians.

Personal Appeals

One of the responsibilities of nationals, missionaries and some speakers is to raise money for their own organizations. They are expected to do this and in some cases their own boards may give them a hard time if they fail to show any financial progress as a result of their conferences. Consequently, any of your guests may make direct or indirect appeals for their special needs that will syphon off funds from your main missionary budget.

As a rule of thumb you can conclude that gifts given privately to one of your guests will be taken directly from your church members' regular contributions to the world missions program of your church. Very few people can handle both. Sometimes they will tell themselves that their special gift will be an "extra" but it very seldom is, and as a result the church budget will invariably suffer.

To avoid this we do a number of things and I remind our guests of these at the briefing:

- We do not officially invite any missionaries or nationals unless we are already supporting their society. We may not be supporting them as individuals but we are supporting one or more of their fellow workers. Whether we are supporting guests personally or not I remind them that their task at our conference is to help us raise money for their colleagues or their society's projects to which we are already committed. They must not make any attempt to raise their own support or get aid for their own projects either in our church or in the homes where they may be staying. As a matter of fact, we expect them to refuse any help that may be offered and if it is foisted upon them, we expect them to turn it in to the church.
- Sometimes we invite guests, knowing ahead of time that they are in need of support — as in the case of new candidates — or that they are involved in a project that our church has already sanctioned and has agreed to help. In these cases I ask our guests to appeal publicly as strongly as they can, but then I do all the money raising — and thus to

some extent control the amount that is raised. Even for an authorized project, it is a "no-no" for an invited guest to accept gifts on the side or to have them diverted directly to his or her own mission. We raise all the funds and all the funds must be channeled through our books.

- When we invite a main speaker who is involved in some missionary work I have found that the best way to give him some form of remuneration is to take on some of his workers or a share in one of his projects. In this way we can give him far more, over a period of time, than we could if we were to give him a mere honorarium of a few hundred dollars. A share in the work generally amounts to several thousand dollars over a period of months or years. Most people with a missionary heart would far rather have you help their work than to help them personally. Sometimes this results in our support of missions and workers that would not normally fit into our missionary policy, but we believe this is a justifiable reason to bend the policy.

It is important to stress the fact that all of these requirements apply to both direct and indirect appeals. Once in a while someone innocently breaks the rules. One year one of our national guests brought an inspiring message and in a sort of aside mentioned — in not more than two sentences — that he was praying for a motorcycle that would cost about a thousand dollars. After the service one of my elders came up and told me that he was giving the money to buy it. Of course I did not refuse, but I was embarrassed because I had a dozen other nationals who also needed things and had no chance to appeal for them.

To our exhibit room, which we reinstated in 1979, we only invite missionaries whose work we are already supporting. In this way there is much less temptation to solicit funds in the exhibit room. A new mission will always interest some people and if it is represented in the exhibit room a person may be enticed into supporting it, even though he may have too many obligations already.

Sometimes one of my dynamic speakers will inspire the people to give to some other good cause that has not been authorized by the church. To avoid having my people come up after the service with names, addresses and gifts, I offset some of this by taking a retiring offering on the spur of the moment for his cause. It is a breach of etiquette on his part to have mentioned it, but at least I have guided my people's giving and kept most of the money going through the channels of The Peoples Church.

To the novice these restrictions may seem harsh and in many churches that are not deeply involved in missions anyway they are unnecessary. But as the shepherd of my flock I feel it is my responsibility to lead my people in their giving and to control the expenditure of their money as a good steward.

Remember that ninety percent of your guests will be harmless in these respects, but it is your duty to protect your people and your church from the other ten percent.

You can cover all of these issues in your briefing and I have found that most of my guests appreciate knowing what we expect from them. Most dedicated people need to know the guidelines because they would be embarrassed if they were to innocently overstep them in some way. They won't, if you are straightforward with them and tell them. Maybe one out of a hundred will knowingly violate all of your requests. If he does, it is generally best not to make an issue of it. Just be sure that you never invite him for another conference. In your church you always have the last word.

Special Emphasis

Finally, I brief my guests to be careful that they do not stress their particular kind of missionary work at the expense of other kinds, or leave the impression that their method alone can evangelize the world.

In my position I deal with most of the methods that are being used and the directors of these missions are nearly all personal friends of mine. Sometimes I am amused, but more often concerned, when I hear them or read their material. They promote their own particular method — literature, radio, television, nationals, foreign students, foreign missionaries, Bibles, schools, hospitals, relief, Christian business and professional people who are not in the country as missionaries, short-term workers, student trips, and so on — but often they talk about it as if it was going to be able to finish the task. It is quite natural for them to do this, but it may lead people to think that other methods are not as good.

The truth is that no one method will ever complete the job. It will probably take all of these systems combined to do it. It should be remembered that no one weapon wins a war by itself. Even with the phenomenal and devastating atomic bombs that were dropped on Japan, it cannot be said that they won the victory. All they did was to immobilize and temporarily frighten the Japanese government. The war was not won until the ground troops moved in and occupied the country. Even then the purpose of the war was not accomplished until the troops could be replaced with an occupational government that was eventually controlled completely by the Japanese. Anything less than this would not be complete victory.

The objective of all missionary work is the establishment of assemblies of believers. It is very seldom that this can be accomplished without the Christian infantry moving in. This is the foreign missionary. God's plan is to establish a church and for this most of the dynamic modern methods must finally rely on the "old fashioned" flesh-and-blood foreign missionary.

Radio needs literature. Literature is helped by radio. Television helps both and they help television. In other words, we all need each other and are foolish to think we can go it alone. Furthermore, we are being proud when we disparage others.

But in the final analysis, after the ground troops have occupied and planted churches the work must be turned over to the nationals who should have been trained by the missionaries. It is only when the occupation troops and government can leave, or turn to new tasks that involve pioneer methods or areas, that we can say any country has been evangelized.

So my briefing to the missionary specialists is, "Promote, extol, and elevate your own work and method, but remember that you still need everybody else because your method can never finish the task alone."

Sometimes I have enough time to brief our guests about all of these things in one session, but even then I keep repeating them before each service, maybe dealing with only one at a time. After a few days have gone by I usually have stressed most of these points two or three times.

4

The Importance of a Missionary Policy

It is not at all important that your church adopt the same policy as our church, or for that matter any other church, but it is very important that you put together some sort of policy by which you regulate your missionary program.

The missionary policy may have many purposes but there are three which stand out in a special way:

- It will be helpful to your missionary committee because it will answer many questions automatically and save the members a great deal of time discussing individual items already covered by the policy.
- It will enable your church to treat all your workers and boards in the same manner without favoring some and not others. If you do not have a policy you will discover that your missionary allotments will be in danger of favoring the people who are good deputational workers and happen to have rather outgoing warm personalities, and this may be done at the expense of some of the greatest missionaries in the world who do not happen to have ability along the lines of deputational work.

  This is particularly important when answering questions that members of the congregation may ask about different projects and missionaries. If you have a policy on how to deal with them, that is generally the only answer the members of your church will need. If you do not have such a policy you will discover that pressure will be brought to bear on the pastor and the missionary committee to favor friends, relatives, and people with great personal charisma.
- A policy will make clear in the minds of your missionaries and boards what they may expect from your church by way of help. If the time should ever come when some of your missionary projects or personnel no longer fall within the description of your missionary policy, it will be very easy for you to write to the people involved and tell them that you

must discontinue your share in their support. They will have difficulty objecting because they already have a copy of your policy and they know that this regulation was not formulated for them in particular.

The following is the policy of The Peoples Church. It has been developed over a period of fifty years at the time of writing. I cannot emphasize too strongly that this is not an example of what your policy should be, but rather an example of the kinds of things you should attempt to cover in your policy.

Missionary Policy of The Peoples Church

1) Each year we hold a World Missions Conference at which time "faith promises" are made for the next twelve months.
2) Speakers are invited on the understanding that they will not solicit names or send appeals to our contributors. Should any gifts be received as a result of the conference, they should be turned over to the church office and a check obtained to cover them.
3) Missionaries are accepted for support with the definite understanding that they will not solicit or accept funds from the adherents of The Peoples Church for their extra needs. These must be secured elsewhere.
4) With very few exceptions, we support missionaries under the societies accredited by the Interdenominational Foreign Mission Association of North America, in order to safeguard the funds with which we are entrusted.
5) Missionaries assigned to us by the various boards are gladly accepted for support, even though we may never have seen them. In addition we accept those from our own church, as God provides the funds.
6) We do not administer the work on any of the fields. We deal directly with the particular board, then leave the board to work with the missionary.
7) We contribute $1,920 a year toward the personal support of each Canadian couple, and we give double support to any of our own young people who have gone to the "field" since 1967. If we are to support over five hundred workers regularly, we cannot provide for extras such as outfits, transportation, and special field needs. Our allowance for national workers varies with the country in which they live.

8) It is our conviction that "The supreme task of the Church is the evangelization of the world." Therefore, we work with the societies that concentrate on reaching the unevangelized people of the earth. "Why should anyone hear the Gospel twice before everyone has heard it once?" (Oswald J. Smith).
9) We differentiate between physical and spiritual needs, and material appeals are emphasized only if they involve a spiritual objective. In recent years we have contributed approximately $200,000 a year to help with physical needs in some of the "disaster" areas of the world. This money has been disbursed by the World Relief Commission, the relief arm of the National Association of Evangelicals. All of this work is done by evangelical missionaries and is accompanied with the proclamation of the message of the gospel. The majority of these funds comes from our television audience.
10) Our promise holds good for twelve months, provided God sends in the funds and is then renewed on the basis of our conference offering.
11) We continue payment of the allowance for a period of one year after the missionary comes home on a regular furlough, and then, if he is not going to return, our responsibility ceases. Our responsibility would also cease if the missionary were to accept a remunerative position with some organization other than his society.
12) Our policy is to support Canadian citizens and national Christian leaders only. Allowances commence in the third quarter of a given year, or whenever the missionary actually leaves for the field thereafter. Remittances are sent to the societies at the end of each quarter.
13) We contribute large sums to foreign literature, believing that "the gospel must first be published among all nations," and that systematic distribution of literature is one of the most effective means of evangelism.
14) We work only with those missions that accept the absolute authority of the Scriptures. Their vision is to evangelize the unreached millions of the earth and bring back the King.
15) We do not give only out of sympathy. Our policy is to hasten the return of the Lord by following His program for this age, which is to preach the gospel in all the world for a witness to all nations and to take out of them a people for His name (Matthew 24:14, Acts 15:14).

16) If we are to meet the regular allowances of our missionaries throughout the year, we cannot take up special offerings for those who visit us from time to time between conferences.
17) We are always glad to pass on special contributions, but we would much rather have our people loyally support the missionaries listed in The Peoples Magazine, for whom we are responsible.
18) Our home missions projects include gifts to the Ontario Bible College, the Yonge Street Mission, The Canadian Home Bible League, The Shantymen's Christian Association, and some other worthy evangelical organizations which seek to reach people in Canada. We also include a subsidy for The Peoples Christian School and The Peoples Ranch.
19) Our television ministry is included in our world missions projects, but income from the television audience more than supports the cost of these programs. They do not have to be financed by the faith promise offering received at the World Missions conference.
20) We share in the support of many of our own people who go out on short-term missionary projects. Most of these are young people on summer programs. We absorb a substantial share in the cost of these with the understanding that the persons involved will not make any attempt to raise additional funds from adherents of The Peoples Church (apart from their own immediate families). Appeals must not be made either directly or by dwelling on needs in a talk to any of our Sunday School classes or groups. Any funds that come from our own people must be considered a part of the total allowance for that particular short-term missionary. The amount for these special workers is determined by the total cost of the trip and the number of weeks involved.

If you do not have a missionary policy, the best way to begin formulating one is to set down on paper the ways in which you are doing your missionary work at the present time. Then your committee can look over this list of principles and decide if this is the route you want to go in the future. In most cases churches discover that the core of a well-formulated missionary policy started simply by putting down what was happening at the time they began to write the policy.

Just as the constitutions of most nations can be amended and the regulations of most organizations altered — so the missionary policy may be up-dated from time to time. We make minor changes in our missionary policy almost every year. New problems come up that have not been covered by the policy and if we find that these are going to be appearing frequently in the future, we attempt to put down in our policy the way in which we will deal with these particular things.

5

A Word about Words

For want of a better expression, most of us have agreed that a person who ministers in another culture is referred to as a missionary and one who ministers in his own country is called a national.

National

If most of my ministry is in Canada, I am a national. I minister in my own country to my own people. When I spend most of my time in any other country I am really a missionary. These names will be attached to me wherever I go. The missionary is still thought of as a missionary even when he is home on furlough and the national is still called a national even though he may be ministering for a short time in a foreign country. The terms "national" and "missionary" have to do with wherever we spend most of our time.

Missionary

Some folk make a big fuss over calling *any* of God's servants missionaries unless we call *all* of them missionaries. I can understand the problem, but I do not appreciate this as a solution. I know that there is a sense in which all workers are missionaries, but it is a fact that there is a difference between the person who works at home and the one who works in some other part of the world or amongst people of some different culture and we need a name by which to distinguish one from the other.

From my observation it would seem that there are many other things that make the missionary's calling different from the local minister's. The missionary nearly always leaves most of his family behind, while very often the pastor works within easy reach of his family. Although his wife and children travel with him the missionary may yet have to suffer separation from his children. They need to be educated and often the other country does not provide the kind of training his children need. The local minister generally does not have to face this sort of separation — certainly not when the children are in the early years of grade school.

When I was in Irian Jaya in 1979, the children were all home for the Christmas break, but early in January they had to be flown out of the jungle for schooling — even the little ones had to say goodbye.

There is a vast difference between a missionary and a local minister. We do not live the same kinds of lives nor do we minister in the same ways, and we do not face the same kinds of personal and family problems that are caused by the difference of our geographical locations. The name "missionary" is a good word that points out the differences in our ministries, and we should use it without apology.

Full-time Worker

"Full-time worker" is another term that suffers needlessly from attack. Of course there is a sense in which all God's people are full-time workers. All of us should be doing whatever we do on a full-time basis for God. But there are some who work in a professional sense — that is, they are dependent upon God's work for their livelihood. The term "full-time worker" only serves to point up this difference. The minister who suggested that there is no difference between his work and the work of his people is kidding himself. The bricklayer or the doctor may be a godly man, but his living does not depend on his godliness. It would continue to be his source of support whether he was godly or devilish.

A minister is not paid for being godly — as if his people were not godly — but if he were to renounce any effort or longing to be godly he would forfeit his salary and his livelihood. It is not a case of anyone being any better or closer to God because he preaches rather than ploughs, but there is a difference between the two, and "full-time worker" points it out.

When I ask young people to volunteer for service, I am not asking for dedication alone. This is important and valid and the thing many people should do. But I am asking for those who will consider some kind of work for God as their life's work and their sole means of survival. That is why I need a word to describe that sort of life. "Full-time worker" does it.

Evangelization

Throughout these pages I have used the word "evangelization" frequently. My definition of this word would include the idea of discipling converts after they have responded to the gospel. The great commission in the New Testament usually means preaching and teaching, "Go ye therefore, and teach all nations, baptizing them in the name of the Father, and of the Son, and of the Holy Ghost; Teaching them to observe all things whatsoever I have commanded you: and, lo, I am with you alway, even unto the end of the world. Amen" (Matthew 28:19-20).

The command of our Lord does not always add the part about teaching, but apparently the apostles thought that discipling was an intrinsic part of evangelism. Wherever they went they preached the gospel and then stayed long enough to teach their converts, who eventually organized themselves into churches, or assemblies of believers, who met on a regular basis in specified places. Sometimes the apostle Paul stayed more than two years to do this.

One of the exciting problems in missionary work today is that we are having a hard time coping with the colossal task of discipling. We are well organized for preaching the gospel, but today the response is so fantastic in some parts of the world that our teaching facilities have been taxed far beyond their capacities. However, the boards — both Western and Third World — are alert to this problem and are making huge strides in the right direction.

In my writing I have used the one word "evangelization," but with an understanding of its full meaning in the Scriptures.

Foreign

The word "foreign" has unfortunate connotations for some of us — as does its synonym "alien." We have a tendency to think of a "foreigner" as someone who may be among us but is not really one of us. Or we imagine that he is strange and in some cases opposed to us or our way of life.

The actual dictionary definition of the word "foreign" would be "*situated* outside one's own country." It is a derivative of a Latin word meaning "outside."

In fact a foreigner is simply someone who lives in some other country. A foreign country is any nation other than our own and a foreign missionary is a missionary that has left his own land and has chosen to serve God in some other place. It is often a better country and many times a larger country. It is foreign only in the respect that it is located somewhere else in the world and may have a different kind of culture or be predominated by another religion.

In no sense should the word "foreign" be construed as being bad, inferior, underprivileged, underdeveloped or primitive. If we insist on thinking about the unfortunate connotations, we would do well to avoid the use of the word altogether in connection with world missions. If we know what it really means and think of it in this way it can be used freely, and we may talk about foreigners, foreign countries and foreign missionaries. I find its use necessary to distinguish between a missionary who works among a different type of person in his own country or uses some type of approach that is different from the general ministry of a pastor. It saves a lot of time to refer to the first group as foreign missionaries and the others as home missionaries. There should be no derogatory implications in the use of either word. I have used the word "foreign" quite freely in these pages.

Conclusion

Each of these words or phrases — national, missionary, full-time worker, or foreign — helps us to say in a breath what it might otherwise take a paragraph to describe. So go ahead and use them. Don't waste God's time and the people's by beating about the bush to describe these different kinds of people or work. Or don't put down the congregation by assuming that they don't have enough intelligence to put these names in their proper theological and scriptural context.

6

Don't Be Afraid of Money

"And now we come to the necessary evil of this service — the offering."

I could hardly believe it was happening, but there he stood on the platform of the Central Methodist Church in downtown Liverpool in the summer of 1953 apologizing for the fact that we could not get on with the important spiritual part of the service until we had done away with this rather dirty business of asking God's people for money with which to support God's work.

It was coronation year in England and I was conducting an evangelistic campaign under the auspices of the Merseyside Youth for Christ. The Methodists had allowed us the use of their spacious downtown church — a sort of "preaching center" where the local people know that they may hear some of the world's better known preachers from time to time. It was the practice each evening to have one of the local clergymen make the intimations (announcements) and ask for the offering.

Youth for Christ had gone all out for this crusade so the expenses were high and we had a rather formidable budget to raise. You can imagine how my heart sank as night after night these dear men of God, the local pastors, apologized for the offering. This kind of thing is generally more pronounced in countries that have had a state church or one that was underwritten by a big landowner and where there was never any pressure put on the people for money.

It is usually unfortunate if a church is supported by a state or one wealthy man, or even a few wealthy people. Any analysis of church finances will show that God's work is not sustained by wealthy Christians, even though we are grateful for those who can give substantially. Most of the money comes from the grass roots people who give a mass of small offerings.

Several times I have tabulated the total of gifts in our church that amount to five thousand dollars or more, and in the area of missionary giving these would total less than a hundred thousand dollars, which is only a small percentage of the one-million-plus that we need to continue our missionary work.

Perhaps I should say here that I take very little personal interest in how much any individual in our church gives. I very rarely even know, unless it is brought to my attention so that I can adequately express appreciation. Even in the tabulation of the large amounts that I have mentioned I never know the names of the people involved — only the numbers and amounts.

This is important, because one of the basic principles in a faith promise offering is that no one will ask for it, either by direct mail or in personal conversation. It is a commitment between a person and God and if it cannot be fulfilled, only God needs an explanation. In our church we do ask our people to attach their name to their promises — not to detract from the fact that the promise is with God alone but for at least three reasons:

- The committee needs a basis upon which to budget the church's involvement in missions during the next year. This can be done if it has an idea of how much the commitment of the people has been. Otherwise, it would not be necessary even to hand in envelopes at all.
- Most people are more likely to take their promise seriously if they have signed it. For many of us it is much easier to forget a blank agreement than it is to forget a signed agreement, and
- Names help our office to verify promises that look suspicious so that we do not count on a large amount from someone who cannot be identified. In a church of our size we always have a few who will be carried away with the faith promise concept and think, "If I don't need cash for this offering, but only my faith in God, then the sky is the limit and I can promise anything."

Of course, in the last case, such a person has completely missed the point that a faith promise should be intelligent — not foolish. There are not many of these, even in a large church, but having a name attached to a promise helps us to avoid counting exceptionally large amounts that come from questionable sources.

One year a promise was made by phone as a result of our television appeal. It came from a local mayor who happened to be a very fine member of the Jewish community. Since it involved a sizeable sum, we simply telephoned his home and quickly learned that the call had come from a prankster.

Applied to any sort of an offering to God, the terms "necessary" and "evil" are not at all scriptural. Any adequate definition of God would show that our gifts are not necessary. Certainly, God does not need us. He could have done the work alone or He would not be God. God does not need Christian workers to help Him with His work. Nor does He need my money to help Him carry out His purpose. The glory of the gospel is not that God needs us, but that in His love and graciousness He has given us the privilege of working with Him: "For we are labourers together with God" (I Corinthians 3:9). The offering is not a necessity but a privilege.

Nor is it evil to ask God's people for support. If it was, the Bible would not say so much about it. The Old Testament gives a great deal of space to the principle of tithing and also the delights of offerings. Although the New Testament principle of giving is different — stewardship rather than tithing (although stewardship may start with and include tithing) — it would be difficult to read it even casually and avoid the many passages that talk about giving, and thus condone the practice of those who remind their people of this responsibility.

One of the longest and most pointed passages on this subject is in Second Corinthians, chapters eight and nine. Chapter eight lays down some of the basic concepts of Christian giving and chapter nine is the biblical basis of a faith promise offering.

7

The Principles of Christian Giving

"Moreover, brethren, we do you to wit of the grace of God bestowed on the churches of Macedonia:

"How that in a great trial of affliction the abundance of their joy and their deep poverty abounded unto the riches of their liberality.

"For to their power, I bear record, yea, and beyond their power they were willing of themselves;

"Praying us with much entreaty that we would receive the gift, and take upon us the fellowship of the ministering to the saints.

"And this they did, not as we hoped, but first gave their own selves to the Lord, and unto us by the will of God.

"Insomuch that we desired Titus, that as he had begun, so he would also finish in you the same grace also.

"Therefore, as ye abound in everything, in faith, and utterance, and knowledge, and in all diligence, and in your love to us, see that ye abound in this grace also" (II Corinthians 8:1-7).

Giving is a Grace (Verses 1 and 7)

In some Bible dictionaries the word "grace" is coupled in the actual heading with the more common word "favor." It is something God bestows on us freely and is emphasized — particularly by Paul — as the antithesis of works. It is the unearned, unmerited favor of God.

There are two aspects to grace. The first is connected with our salvation, "By grace are ye saved" (Ephesians 2:8). The second has to do with the benefits we receive freely from God subsequent to or as a result of our salvation. In both cases "grace" in the Scriptures generally involves not only the favor of God but also the power that first, produces a child of God, and second, helps us to live the sort of life we are expected to live.

In this chapter Paul lists five other graces all in one verse — faith, utterance, knowledge, diligence and love, and then concludes by adding to this list the grace of giving — "see that ye abound to this grace also" (II Corinthians 8:7).

Most of us would accept these other powers as graces, but have difficulty in thinking of giving in the same category. Paul suggests that the power to give is a result of God's grace. It is a favor He bestows on us. He allows us to help Him with His work by giving.

Of course this is the pattern of most of the miracles God performs. Although He is going to interrupt human affairs or physical laws in order to perform a wonder, God often lets people participate in the miracle in some small way.

God turned the rod into a serpent, but He let Moses cast it on the ground. God parted the waters of the Red Sea, but Moses was allowed to lift up his rod and stretch out his hand over the sea. God destroyed the walls of Jericho, but the people participated by marching around them first. Elisha was about to ask God to multiply a bit of oil so that a widow and her two sons could sell it and pay their debt, but God allowed this little family of poor people to share in the miracle by going out and collecting pots to contain the miraculous oil.

In the miracles of Jesus people were often permitted to share. When He turned water into wine, Jesus asked the people to fill the containers with water. When He fed the five thousand a little boy shared by giving his lunch and the disciples were allowed to distribute the miraculous bread and fish. Before Jesus called Lazarus from the grave He asked the men to move the stone that covered the entrance, and after Lazarus came back to life it was the people who removed the grave clothes.

There is no doubt that in all of these cases God could have done what He let people do, but in His grace human beings were favored by being allowed to participate in the work of God.

God could evangelize the world without our gifts, but He permits us to participate by giving — sometimes our lives, always our prayers, and continually our gifts. Giving is one of the graces of the Christian life.

What's Left May Be More Important Than What's Given (Verse 2)

What impressed the apostle about the Christians in Macedonia was that they gave liberally despite the fact that they themselves were very poor. Paul was only doing what his Master had done before him. He paid more attention to what was left than to what was given. When Jesus watched the people giving in the temple

He was moved by the widow who threw in two mites — less than the price of a sparrow. Others had given but it hadn't hurt them. They had plenty left. This woman gave out of her poverty and she had nothing left.

Our dear folk in The Peoples Church give very large offerings for missions — they could be included among the well-known giving churches of North America. In 1978 they promised $1,488,912 for world missions alone out of a total budget of little more than three million dollars, which included the tuition fees of an elementary and high school totaling about six hundred and fifty students, and the cost of a television network that realized over $900,000, leaving about $800,000 for the actual operation of the church. This means that the church adherents gave nearly one and a half million dollars for missions and less than a million for the local church. This is fairly good giving.

But has it hurt any of us? A few to be sure. There are some who have sacrificed and have hurt themselves by their giving to God. But for most of us in The Peoples Church this is not so. On Sunday morning our ladies still choose a dress from a stock of several. Our men decide on which of several suits to wear — in a world where an appalling number have one outfit or less. We go to breakfast with the big decision as to what to eat with several choices — in a world where millions had no breakfast and thousands died of starvation while we were sleeping. When we go to church some of us must choose between two and sometimes three cars, and very often end up crowding the church parking lot with cars with only one person in each. And on and on the choices go in our affluent society, where a few of us even have the audacity to think that we have sacrificed to give substantially to missions, when really we haven't even begun to hurt. We have only scratched the surface.

Fried Chicken and Sterling Silver

I was asked to dinner at the home of a very lovely Christian woman in a great American city. Several missionaries were there with me. We had been participating in a missionary convention in one of the local churches. The hostess was apparently wealthy, and it was a beautiful home, furnished magnificently. We sat down to a table set with sterling silver and burdened with food fit for a banquet.

The dear woman had just returned from Palestine, and in the course of her tour she had seen the orphans of the Holy Land — frail, hungry, pathetic. She described them to us, and it was obvious that she had a great burden for them. I shall never forget what she said, and how she said it: "My heart went out to those hungry little boys and girls who had never heard the gospel. Oh, that we could tell them about Jesus! Mr. Smith, would you please pass the fried chicken?" And as I passed the chicken a tear ran down her cheek and fell on a sterling silver spoon.

I do not condemn this dear soul, because she is just one of thousands of us in the homeland who sit in the lap of luxury and talk about the need of the heathen. Here we are in the nominally Christian countries surrounded on all sides by things we do not need, and we seem to feel that Almighty God should feel highly honored because we have given Him a few dollars.

Coffee Breaks

In this country nearly everyone has a "coffee break" in the morning and afternoon. We have more than fifteen hundred adult givers in the church. Coffee costs twenty-five or thirty cents a cup. If we would add the same amount to our missionary giving as we spend for our daily "coffee breaks" the total in a year's time would be at least $273,750.

If we were to add to that the cost of radios, rugs, jewelry, clothes, etc., that are in the luxury class, the sky would be the limit. I am not trying to say that we should give up our "coffee breaks" or afternoon teas, nor that we should do without the luxuries of life, but I do think we should do at least as much for the cause of Christ as we do for our own comfort.

How to Decide What Should Be Given (Verse 3)

Intelligent givings should be based upon what anyone, including ourselves, knows we should be able to give considering our financial situations in life. Faith promise giving should reach out to attempt *more* than this, and then trust God to enable us to do it. The Macedonians had given "to their power I bear record, yea, and beyond their power" (II Corinthians 8:3).

The New International Version says, "As much as they were able, and even beyond their ability."

The New American Standard Version puts it, "According to their ability, and beyond their ability."

Good News for Modern Man, to some extent a paraphrase, suggests, "As much as they were able, and even more than that."

The Living Bible translates thought for thought as opposed to word for word as follows, "They gave not only what they could afford, but far more."

J.B. Phillips in his presentation of *Letters to Young Churches* paraphrases in this way, "To the limit of their means, yea and beyond their means."

The New International Commentary of the New Testament suggests two meanings, "In accordance with their ability, I testify, indeed contrary to their ability" and "according to their means, as I can testify, and beyond their means."

Matthew Henry's Commentary is very clear, "As much as could well be expected from them, if not more."

Even our governments tax us in accordance with what they feel we should be able to afford. They assume that if a person lives in a given financial bracket, then that person can be expected to pay a certain percentage of his income to help with the operation of his country. Most of us fuss a great deal over the details and ramifications of taxation, but we accept the principle in general.

There are some respects in which the Old Testament law of tithing is based on the taxation principle. It is assumed that a reasonable percentage of our income should be set aside to help support the Lord's work. Ten percent was an arbitrary amount that was established by God. It was not considered in the same class as an offering, because it was not something a Jewish man possessed which he then gave to God. It was an amount that already belonged to God, and if it was withheld, it was as if a person had actually robbed God (Mal. 3:8-10).

The Old Testament teaches that it is possible to make an assessment of how much an individual can reasonably be expected to give to the Lord's work. This passage in Corinthians is probably based on this assumption. My "power" to give is something that I can work out on a simple calculator. It does not require faith because it is something I already hold in my hand and can see. Some faith may be involved in how I will be able to get by on the ninety percent that is left, but the giving itself is a combination of mathematics and will. I calculate what I should do and then I do it.

Going beyond my "power" taxes the resources of my faith. It means a commitment to God of resources that I cannot see. This may involve giving more than could be expected of what I have in my possession and then trusting God to supply my personal needs in the months that lie ahead. Or it might mean promising God an amount, in the months ahead, that is more than my calculator indicates — and then trusting God to make it possible to fulfill my commitment.

In these chapters in Second Corinthians the latter of these two plans seems to be the one that describes the faith promise offering. Apparently, it involved a full year. There was a commitment of intent first, and later there was the performance of that intent (II Corinthians 8:10-11). This is the kind of offering Paul talks about in the next chapter. Chapter eight gives the example of how this worked in Macedonia and based on this success, Paul asked the Corinthians to make a commitment in advance of money or materials that would be needed for the saints in Jerusalem, probably during and certainly by the end of twelve months.

This part of the principle of a faith promise offering means that we should start thinking about an amount that would be possible for us. Then we should lift our faith to some impossible objective — impossible, not because it is utterly foolish and way beyond what might be expected in an extreme form, but impossible because it is beyond our sight, more than what might be expected, beyond the limit of our normal resources, more than we can afford, or beyond our known means.

But our promise is related to our means. That's what keeps it from being foolish. A faith promise involves trusting God for an amount that we do not have, cannot see and therefore must depend upon God to enable us to give. When we discuss chapter nine we will talk about how God usually makes it possble for us to give the impossible.

We Should Initiate Our Own Giving (Verse 4)

In most of our assemblies the giving must be stimulated and urged by the leadership. The apostle Paul was not the least bit backward about doing this. He never apologized for the offering. He promoted and organized it. However, in the case of the Macedonians they seemed to have responded to the need quite spontaneously and had to plead with Paul to accept it.

Needless to say, the apostle did accept their gifts, but he was impressed, if not amazed, at the willingness of these Macedonian Christians. Obviously, this was not normal for the first century churches or in his own ministry. He had already organized the way in which the Corinthians were to be asked to give and he is quick to use the example of the Macedonians to provoke them to a large response. The offering at Corinth was organized, promoted by the brethren who were sent on ahead, and asked for in a very forthright manner.

There are still a few organizations that never ask for support. This is probably due to the concept that was behind the early Faith Missions. That is, they chose to pray about their needs and then trust God to send in the necessary funds. Most of this resulted from the example of George Muller of Bristol who raised money for his orphanage by staying on his knees and and asking God rather than people. I have seen his office and the indentations on the hardwood floor where he used to kneel.

My heart was warmed as I stood there and re-dedicated my own life to God, but I must remember that this was a special ministry into which God led this dear saint. Most of the Bible's teaching indicates that giving involves talking to both man and God — not only God.

By far the majority of Faith Missions not only tell people about their needs, but through their literature and deputational workers ask God's people to support them. Some of those, if not all, who do not ask for funds directly do publish their needs in some form — if only by being represented at a missions conference. I know of very few who run this department of their work entirely from their "prayer closets."

The name "Faith Mission" usually helps us to distinguish between a denominationally-based mission and an interdenominational or independent mission. The word "faith" in this context really applies to both kinds of boards. Independents and denominations must ultimately exert faith if their work is to continue. In the case of Faith Missions we sometimes use the name meaning that they do not have the backing of a given group of churches from whom they might expect support and therefore, they must have faith that God will raise up churches that will feel led to support them. However, "Faith Mission" rarely means that they do not go to the people in some manner and ask for help — even if all they may do is express their needs.

The ideal is for God's people to be like the Christians in the Macedonian Church — that is, to give without urging, then beg some cause to accept their gifts. The fact is that this is a very rare exception and was a surprise to the apostle Paul. For this reason he felt led to ask the other churches for help.

Giving Must Be Preceded by Living (Verse 4)

This verse zeros in on the core of New Testament giving. It is essential that the giving of our money — or, for that matter, anything else we have — must be preceded by the complete dedication of ourselves to God, "I beseech you therefore, brethren, by the mercies of God, that ye present your bodies a living sacrifice, holy, acceptable unto God, which is your reasonable service" (Romans 12:1).

When the rich young ruler came to Jesus and asked what he should do to have eternal life, I think he expected Jesus to ask him for a major contribution of some kind. What a shock it must have been for him when the Master told him to sell everything and give to the poor, and then he could follow Jesus. But what an even greater jolt it must have been to the disciples who may have seen in this rich man the financial backing that might get the cause of Christ launched. The words of Jesus dashed these hopes to the ground.

But this is the principle: Jesus asks for the unreserved dedication of His people, and only after we have given this does He give us the privilege of giving our money, goods, time or talent. It follows that if God has me, He has my possessions. By my consecration everything I am or own belongs to God. That makes me a steward — one who handles his master's possessions. A steward never spends his own money — he spends his master's. He never uses his own talent — he uses his master's. He doesn't give his own time — he gives his master's.

In the Old Testament the question of giving should be phrased this way: "How much of my money should I give to God?" The answer is ten percent. In the New Testament the question is drastically different: "How much of God's money should I keep for myself in order to pay the expenses of living?"

I said it once before. Let me repeat it in this context. The Old

Testament system of giving was called tithing. The New Testament system is stewardship. This may include tithing, and that is a good place for a young convert to start, but stewardship is much more comprehensive.

The rest of chapter eight deals with some of the logistics of the offering. Paul sent Titus and two other well-known brethren. There was a full year involved, probably preceded by a commitment, "a readiness to will," and followed perhaps a year later by the completion of the offering, "perform the doing of it."

8

The Faith Promise

"For as touching the ministering to the saints, it is superfluous for me to write to you:

"For I know the forwardness of your mind, for which I boast of you to them of Macedonia, that Achaia was ready a year ago; and your zeal hath provoked very many.

"Yet have I sent the brethren, lest our boasting of you should be in vain in this behalf; that, as I said, ye may be ready:

"Lest haply if they of Macedonia come with me, and find you unprepared, we (that we say not, ye) should be ashamed in this same confident boasting.

"Therefore I thought it necessary to exhort the brethren, that they would go before unto you, and make up beforehand your bounty, whereof ye had notice before, that the same might be ready, as a matter of bounty, and not as of covetousness.

"But this I say, He which soweth sparingly shall reap also sparingly; and he which soweth bountifully shall reap also bountifully.

"Every man according as he purposeth in his heart, so let him give; not grudgingly, or of necessity: for God loveth a cheerful giver" (II Corinthians 9:1-7).

The first faith promise offering in our times was probably organized by a Presbyterian minister. Dr. A.B. Simpson founded the Christian and Missionary Alliance denomination — although a denomination was not a part of his original vision. Dr. Simpson was greatly concerned about world evangelization and the older Alliance churches existed primarily to promote and support foreign missions.

To do this they had a missionary convention every year at which their people were urged to designate a large percentage of their total giving to missions. They still do this. The offering is a commitment of what the people will trust God to enable them to do in the next twelve months and it is generally called a pledge. The Christian and Missionary Alliance churches established the system and led the way for the rest of us in this kind of giving for missions.

One of the revolutionary things about the Alliance conventions was that they dared to urge their people to give directly to missions. They were willing to take this sort of risk, knowing that more might be designated for missions than for the local work. To this day the majority of churches are not willing to take this chance. That is why world missions is promoted, but is included in the total budget of the local church — so that a committee can control or recommend the percentage that should be given for missions. Better that it is done this way than not at all, but better still to allow each person to be led by the Holy Spirit to give to whatever area of God's work he wishes.

The objection, of course, is that the local work may suffer. My experience over fifty years of "faith promise" giving directly for missions has been that as our missionary budget rises our local income increases. This means that we have to be very careful with our local spending, and that's why we go functional in our buildings rather than plush. This has also been the experience of hundreds of other churches that have dared to adopt the faith promise system of giving for missions.

My father, Dr. Oswald J. Smith, was introduced to this method when he pastored the Alliance Church in Toronto during the early twenties. He describes it in these words: "I became pastor of a church that knew how to give in a way that I had never known.

"I commenced my pastorate on the first Sunday of January. The church was holding its Annual Missionary Convention. Now I knew nothing about a convention. I had never seen one in all my life, so I just sat on the platform and watched."[1]

The Alliance method of raising money for missions captured father's imagination, but he was bothered by their use of the word "pledge." Of course, to them it simply involved a promise to God, but during his days as a Presbyterian minister father recalled that the word sometimes had connotations that some folk didn't like. In some churches the pledge had become a sort of contract between a person and the church. It could be asked for if it had not been paid. An elder might even be assigned to call on someone at home in order to point out their unpaid balance. Many churches practiced the policy of sending out a semi-annual or

---

[1] Smith, Oswald J., *The Challenge of Missions,* (Marshall, Morgan & Scott, London, 1976) p. 59.

quarterly statement that showed how the accounts of their members stood — whether they had paid their pledge or not.

Some of these were rather extreme measures and did not apply to all Presbyterian churches, but throughout most denominations some of these things were associated with the idea of a pledge. My father searched for some word that would express the concept that had always been used in the Christian and Missionary Alliance churches — a word to take the place of "pledge."

He concluded that the two words "faith promise" would be ideal. This would retain the missionary offering concept of the Alliance people and eliminate the unfortunate connotations of the word "pledge." Whether or not this was actually originated by father I do not know. However, it is safe to say that it was his ministry that made the evangelical world familiar with the expression "faith promise." Very few of the tracts or booklets that have been written on the subject can complete their topic without reference at some point to Dr. Oswald J. Smith.

There are a few people, knowing little about a faith promise, who think that this is just another good gimmick to raise a lot of money. If that's all it was, I would still use it for the cause of missions. I am in favor of any legitimate means of urging Christians to give to God's work. However, faith promise giving has a very solid basis in the Scriptures. We have already noted some of this in chapter eight of *Second Corinthians*. But chapter nine is more specific.

The Purpose of This Offering (Verse 1)

This offering was not received in order to send missionaries out to preach the gospel. It was for the suffering and impoverished Christians in the church at Jerusalem. It may have been persecution that made it difficult for them to make a living, but at any rate they needed help. Paul and others undertook to raise an offering that would give them relief.

It was a missionary offering in the sense that it was not raised for the needs of the local church. It was carried to Jerusalem and used for others. Regardless of its use, the method remains valid. It does not have to be restricted to world missions. It can be used for buildings, schools, church operation, etc. But in our times it has been most closely associated with missions.

Let's Provoke Someone (Verse 2)

The intriguing words to me are "Your zeal hath provoked very many." There are two ways that we can provoke people. Often we do things that make them angry. This is not what Paul is talking about. Rather, we can produce something in our lives or our churches, by the grace of God, that captures the imagination of others and inspires them to reach for higher goals themselves.

Paul prayed for the kind of offering that would make all the other churches look in their direction and say "If Macedonia and Corinth can do that, think what we should be doing." All of us should ask God to help us live the kind of life and be the sort of church that provokes others to stretch out further for God.

One of the best results of a great faith promise offering in a big church is that it will inspire scores of other churches to do the same thing, therefore the aggregate offering of the "provoked" churches could be far greater than that of the one big church.

Good Results Require Detailed Organization (Verses 3-5)

This passage describes the manner in which Paul organized the offering. It was not done on the spur of the moment. He did not wait until he got there himself and then have the baskets passed for whatever cash or goods the people might give. But rather he planned the whole thing carefully over a period of months. The apostle did his homework, then expected God to bless and bring the necessary results.

Granted, we can do very little of the real work of the Kingdom. We cannot save people, nor fill them with the Holy Spirit, nor force them to give a substantial offering. But we can plan a meeting. We can explain who the Holy Spirit is. We can organize the logistics of an offering, and it would appear that God expects us to do these things, and do them thoroughly and energetically, knowing at the same time that it is God who does the big, essential things.

Three men were sent to Corinth to finalize the offering that was to be received when Paul arrived, perhaps months later, before it was to be carried to Jerusalem. We know that Titus was one of these and the others are not named. The people in the church knew about the need even before these three men arrived. Thus the organization included at least three parts: phase one — advance notice; phase two — arrival of the brethren to finalize the commitments, and phase three — the offering to be received by Paul when he arrived. One of the most scholarly commentaries on this book says about this passage: "It was not so much a question of their readiness to give, but rather of the need for efficient planning to get the money in."[2]

Paul Held a Pep Rally

Before they left for Corinth Paul took time to explain his plans to the brethren. But in doing so the Bible says that he "exhorted" them. Some of the other versions used the word "urged." In either case Paul was pressing home his point strongly. He wanted them not only to understand the plan, but to get excited about the possibilities. In this spirit they would be able to arouse the interest of the Corinthians.

What Did The Brethren Do?

The whole import of the passage is that these three men did not go about actually collecting cash or goods. They were there to find out what people were planning to give when the time arrived. They went to the assembly or maybe to the Christians' homes to tabulate what the offering was actually going to be.

Perhaps Mr. Jones was a wheat farmer. When the men knocked on his door he was not prepared to give, but when he learned that he had several months before the offering was needed, and that all these men wanted to know was how much he believed God would enable him to give when the time came, he became interested. Now they were talking about something he could do.

Jones may have thought a little bit about who he was and what a man like him could promise. "I own ten acres of corn on my farm outside of Corinth. It's quite small at this time of year, but when it's harvested, I'll give the proceeds to this offering." Perhaps Titus wrote this information on some first century faith promise tablet with a stylus and the trio left rejoicing at the faithfulness of God and the generosity of Mr. Jones.

But as a matter of fact, they did not have a thing — except a promise based on someone's confidence in the power of God to

---

[2]Hughes, Philp E., *The New International Commentary on the New Testament, Second Epistle to the Corinthians,* (Eerdmans, Grand Rapids, Mich., 1962) p. 325.

help him keep it. The corn was still green. Worms might destroy it before harvest time. The bottom might fall out of the market and make it impossible to sell. Maybe Jones would be too ill to work by then, or he might even be dead. All he had really said was this: "In dependence upon God I will endeavor to give the proceeds of a ten-acre field of corn." Mr. Jones had made one of the first faith promises.

Mr. Brown may have been a cattle rancher. When the elders arrived at his home perhaps he was a bit embarrassed because at this time of year he was always low on cash. You can imagine how happy he was to learn that at this juncture they were not expecting cash. All they wanted was to tabulate Brown's expectations, his hopes, his faith in God.

"Well then, that's easy. Tell you what I'll do. I have a cow that will soon be having a calf. It will be several months yet, but if all goes well and the calf is born as expected, I'll sell it and contribute the proceeds." Once again Titus wrote rapidly on his tablet — "Brown, one calf."

And the calf was not even born yet. Maybe it would be stillborn. The mother might die before it was born. Brown might not be able to sell it. But what was his promise? "In dependence upon God I will endeavor to give the proceeds from the sale of one calf to the work of God," and a second faith promise had been made.

Finally, Titus and his two friends knocked on Mr. Smith's door. Now Smith was a big-time developer. He was almost finished with a shopping center on the east side of town and he had made a bid on the proposed Corinth Subway System. But he had no cash.

There are two kinds of people who very seldom have any money available — poor people for obvious reasons, and very wealthy people who have everything invested. Most eminently successful folk make sure that every spare dollar is gaining interest all the time, and do not keep much cash around.

This, of course, was Smith's first response to the brethren. Everything was tied up — caught at a bad time, etc. Once again they patiently explained the nature of the offering. "You don't need any cash. This is not a pledge between you and some church. No one will ever ask you for it personally. It's between you and God. If for some reason you suffer a financial reverse, the only explanation you will have to give is to God. We are asking you to make a promise based on who you are and your faith in the power of God — your dependence upon God. We may drop you a note to thank you for making the promise and when Paul gets to Corinth in a few months he'll announce to the church that it's time to take the money to the poor Christians in Jerusalem. If, at that time, you are unable to give, no one will ever know it except you and God. We will not ask you for it in person."

"Under those conditions here's what I am going to trust God to enable me to do: if the transaction with the shopping center works out all right and I don't lose my shirt on it, and if I get the subway contract, in dependence upon God I will endeavor to give five hundred denarii (about $8,000)."

Out came the stylus again and Smith's faith promise was recorded. As the three men walked down the street they rejoiced — ten acres of corn, one calf and five hundred denarii. But all they really had was three promises — the commitment of three men who had said in essence that if God made it possible for them to secure this money they would give it to Paul for the Jerusalem Christians.

The Reaping of Faith — Not Cash (Verse 6)

The reward that this verse offered was related to the commitment of these people. The cash offering had not even been received at this time. All the people had done was to make a promise based on their faith in God to enable them to keep it. In its proper context the verse should read: "But this I say, He who commits himself with reserve can expect to reap in accordance with his promise. He who promises with a big heart and a deep confidence in God will reap in proportion to his promise. It all depends upon who you are and what your station in life may be and upon how great is your faith in God to help a person like you to fulfill your promise."

The "Golden Text" of Faith Promises (Verse 7)

The seventh verse sums it all up by reminding the Corinthians that they should give relative to what they had in their hearts. There was no salary in their hearts, no bank accounts and no cash. The only thing that any of us have in our hearts that can be the basis of an offering is faith in God which gives us a horizon of purpose that is beyond our dreams.

Three Roads to a Financial Miracle

Once the promise has been made to give God something that is not already in our possession and may depend upon a great many unseen things that could happen in the future, how does God enable us to give the money and keep the promise?

As I look back over my own life, my years in The Peoples Church and my experience in scores of other missionary conferences, I can boil the answer down to three major ways that I have seen the faith promise of thousands of people miraculously made possible by God.

- *Moonlighting for Missions.* Some years ago one of my elders came to me and asked for special prayer. I assumed that he was ill or was facing a critical problem in some other area of his life. When I questioned him he said that there was no great problem; he just wanted to keep a faith promise he had made. However, when he told me the amount, I thought he had made a very unrealistic commitment.

He had filled in an envelope and said that in dependence upon God he would endeavor to give ten thousand dollars to the world missions work of The Peoples Church during the next twelve months. Now there were a few people in our church who could give that much money, but Henry was not one of them. He was over seventy years of age and was retired on a very small pension. I felt that it was quite foolish for a person in his financial bracket to expect God to enable him to give ten thousand dollars to missions. I was about to point this out to him when he told me his plan.

"I can live adequately on my pension. However, I am in excellent health despite my age, and I am going to find a job and work for missions. Whatever I make over and above my pension is already committed to this year's missionary offering, and I believe I am still strong enough to earn at least ten thousand dollars or more. Pastor, I want you to pray that I will find a job and that God will keep me in good health."

That day Henry and I made a sort of covenant: I would pray, he would work, and God would get the money. For more than seven years now Henry has been able to give in excess of ten thousand dollars per year. Generally, he gives it to me in person — a thousand dollars at a time.

But, you protest, that isn't a miracle at all. The man just

worked for his money. Anyone can do that. Yes, anyone in similar circumstances could get an extra job and work for missions. But how many do? You see, that's the first miracle — that he did it at all! After a lifetime of work he had every right to retire and enjoy his last years. But as far as joy is concerned Henry is much happier than most of the retired people I know. He is not just waiting around to die. He is living an extremely fulfilled, active and meaningful life. At his age a lot of folk do not have this option. They are unable to work for many different reasons and God knows all about it. What a miracle, that this man was not only able, but willing.

The second miracle in this is that Henry got a job. Usually, this is very difficult or virtually impossible for people over seventy. And the third miracle is that God kept him in good health for at least seven years.

Sometimes God performs a financial miracle in our lives by enabling us to get a second job, or in some way earn additional money that makes it possible for us to keep our faith promise. We have been able to "moonlight for missions."

- *Save here and spend there.* For others, the miracle happens when God shows us some areas of our lives where we can cut back on our regular spending so that we will have enough to overspend for world missions. This is a valid procedure and we do it in many areas of our lives.

I play golf rather badly. As a matter of fact I really only need about five clubs to play the kind of game I do — one wood, three irons and a putter. Going through the production of choosing from a full set of clubs in an elaborate bag doesn't really make all that much difference, but when I do play golf I use the works — every club, an extra putter and an umbrella as well.

Sometimes when I return from the game and go to put away the big bag and many clubs, my wife will ask, "Why do you spend all that money on your golf game? You know your game is bad and that four or five clubs wrapped in a piece of canvas is all you need. Why spend the extra money?"

And the question is valid, but so is my answer, "I don't smoke, I don't drink, I don't even dance, and I figure that if I save all that money in those areas of my life, I have a right to spend more than is necessary on my golf game. I'm not interested in those other things, and for me they are no big problem, but I do like golf.

All I'm doing is saving in one area so that I will be able to spend in another."

Sometimes my wife spends more money on clothes than I think she should. She knows what our income is and, therefore, she must be aware of the fact that the Smith household should live within the confines of our own financial bracket in every area. When I question her about spending too much for clothes, she throws my answer right back at me, "I don't smoke . . . etc."

For some Christians the overspending is on cars, houses, food, furniture, hobbies, etc. They feel that this is legitimate. I can squeeze here and stretch there, cut back here and add there, save here and spend there.

When this principle is applied to a faith promise offering it is a miracle — first that we are willing to do for world missions what we have always done for our golf game, our clothes or our vacations. The second miracle is that instead of spending the extra money on ourselves we are led by the Holy Spirit to give it to others.

I am not suggesting that we should not apply this principle of "saving here to spend there" on these other areas of our lives, but only that we at least put world missions in the same class — that is, something that excites and concerns us so much that we are willing to save in some areas as a response to our Lord's command. Faith promises can be kept by "saving here to spend there" and this is indeed a financial miracle.

• *Money from Nowhere.* I have put this last because it is less common than the first two miracles, but also to emphasize the fact that God does sometimes provide the money for missions from a totally unexpected source — as if He just dropped it into our laps. Many of our people have been able to complete their commitment because they received an inheritance that was not expected. Sometimes it comes in the payment of a bad debt that had long since been written off. Lots of folk have received increases in salary that were not normal in their kind of work. A few — very few — have received money in the mail, as if from nowhere.

In 1975-76 we decided to build a new high school that was urgently needed. We have close to seven hundred students in our Christian schools from pre-kindergarten through grade thirteen. The new building was going to cost well over a million dollars. The leadership people of the school asked me to make an appeal to our school parents to give substantially in the form of promises that should be completed within six months.

I was sitting on the platform at some academy function awaiting the time to make the appeal. I had decided what my approach should be: "Your children attend this school, therefore, you have a greater obligation than anyone to make major contributions," and so on. While I was thinking these things the Holy Spirit spoke to me. It was not in an audible voice, but a sort of response of my heart to God's Spirit. He was saying that before I could ask other parents to give, I should give myself. My daughter was one of those students.

This seemed fairly logical, and in what I thought was a generous spirit, I determined to give fifty dollars. No sooner had this thought come into my mind than that inner voice spoke again: "Paul, fifty dollars won't do. Promise a thousand." I argued a little longer — pointing out to God how heavy my commitments were and that I didn't have an extra thousand dollars, but I lost the debate, and started my appeal to the other parents by telling them that God had led me to promise a thousand dollars. Where I would get it I did not know, and at this juncture I hadn't even discussed it with my wife. I knew we didn't have it, but I believed that somehow God would provide it.

The following day I received a rough draft of our financial statement for the past year. In the course of studying it and looking for any substantial changes from the figures of former years, I noticed one very minor detail. My salary was a few dollars lower than it had been the year before, despite the fact that I had received a raise. It didn't upset me at all. I knew that there could have been tax deductions or changes in some of the benefits that would easily explain the difference. However, I knew that some of the members of my board might question it, so I needed to know the answer.

My business administrator came to my office two days later with the answer. It was one of those bad news and good news things. The bad news — they had made a mistake while putting the payroll on computer and some wrong information about my salary had been fed into it. The good news — that the church owed me more than two thousand dollars in back salary!

When I received that check, I sat down and wrote my own check in the amount of one thousand dollars for the school building. I had been able to keep my promise in full within five days after I made it. To me that was indeed a financial miracle of the first magnitude.

Now, this sort of dramatic answer does not happen in most cases, but it is not an isolated experience. Over the years I have talked to many people who did experience this kind of dramatic response to their faith promise.

9

The Same Thing Another Way

To put the same thing in another way, the method by which we can give substantially to world missions is not with cash but with credit. We are very seldom able to pay for the big important things in life with cash. In most cases, if it were not for credit we could not have many of the things we own.

We buy our homes on credit. If we were to wait until we had saved sufficient cash to pay for a home completely, we could wait in vain. It could take well over $25,000 to buy a small home in almost any North American city. How many of us have ever been able to accumulate that much cash at one time? It would be an impossibility for most of us, but many people have a home. How do we do it? We go to a bank, a mortgage company, or sometimes an individual, and borrow the money, and promise to pay it back in monthly installments during the next twenty or twenty-five years.

We do the same thing when we buy a car, and many people buy a great many other things in the same way. If you were to take from the average American or Canadian family the things they are "buying" on credit, you could leave them in the street with no furniture and perhaps without clothes on their backs.

What are we actually doing when we take a mortgage on a home or finance a car? We are obligating ourselves for a period of months or years to a bank so that we can have the buying power of a large sum of money. Why do we do it? Because we think material things are important. We are willing to obligate ourselves to pay for them.

The question I ask my people is: How important do you consider the work of God? the task of world evangelization? Have you ever taken out credit in the bank of Heaven? Have you ever obligated yourself to God to such an extent that you have been able to do something really big? As long as you try to pay for missions with the cash on hand, your share of the job will never be done. No one has that much cash; but if you will obligate yourself to God, in faith, over a period of twelve months, and promise to give a specified amount month by month during that period, you will be amazed at what you can do.

We receive an offering for missions once a year in The Peoples Church. It is not a cash offering, nor is it a pledge offering. It is not cash, because our people could never give enough cash at any one time to enable us to meet our obligations. It is not a pledge, because a pledge is usually made to a church, and eventually someone from the church may try to collect it.

It is a faith promise offering. Our missionary envelope reads: "In dependence upon God I will endeavor to give month by month . . ." and there is a place to mark the monthly amount on the side of the envelope. We write to everyone who has filled in an envelope and tell them how and where to send their money, but from that point on the transaction is between the individual and God. We never check up to see if the amount has been paid.

Thus the people have not made a pledge to the church, but a faith promise to God, and they trust Him to enable them to pay it. This is the kind of offering the apostle Paul received from the Corinthians. He sent men "beforehand" to make up a "bounty," and he urged them to give, "Every man as he purposeth in his heart" (II Corinthians 9:7). He did not ask for cash. He asked them to make a decision in their own hearts about how much they would be able to give between the time the messengers were sent and the time he arrived.

This is the great New Testament principle of giving that we have tried to put across to our people in The Peoples Church. This is why so many of them have been able to support their own missionary. With cash they could never do it, but with a faith promise they can.

The support of a missionary can be broken up in many different ways. That is why you get such a variety of figures when you ask how much it costs. Generally speaking the support of each individual missionary is divided into "personal" and "service." The personal support is the salary received on the field. The service support may include a great many other things depending on the financial policy of the particular mission. Usually it includes furlough allowance, passage money for the furlough, upkeep on the mission station, supplies necessary for the work, and other items. If a man is married, his wife usually gets the same allowance and service support. If they have children, they receive an allowance for each child.

Thus the answer to your question might be five hundred dollars or fifteen thousand dollars. Both answers could be correct. The first might be the share your church gives to the support of one missionary. The second might be the total support of a missionary family. In many missions this would be low. In others it could be a little high.

In The Peoples Church at the present time we assume responsibility to share in the support of a missionary to the extent of $960 per year. In the case of a couple this would be doubled and if the people involved were adherents of The Peoples Church it would be doubled again. This would represent our support of Canadian foreign missionaries.

Nationals come under a different scale and their support varies a great deal depending upon where they are working. We do this for several reasons. It puts the support of a missionary within the grasp of the average Christian. When an individual or a class in the church support their own missionaries in this way, it makes world evangelization a personal matter. They know their missionaries. They can correspond with them and pray for them as individuals. This method also spreads the interest of our people around the world, instead of concentrating it on one field. They have a world vision.

However, even our share in the support of a missionary could never be assumed by the ordinary businessman if it had to be done on a cash basis; but when he looks forward a year, and makes a faith promise to God to pay a specific amount month by month, just as he pays the mortgage on his home, he discovers that he can accomplish things for God that otherwise would be an impossibility.

Ask yourself, your friends, your people:
Have you ever made a faith promise? Have you ever managed to do something big for the cause of world evangelization? Have you ever dreamed of supporting your own missionary? You can do it, if you will make a faith promise to God. Obligate yourself to Him, just as you have obligated yourself to the bank. When it is time to pay your bills, pay God first. Take it off the top of your income at the beginning of the month. If you take it off the bottom there will be nothing left for God.

Jesus said, "But seek ye first the kingdom of God, and His righteousness; and all these things shall be added unto you" (Matthew 6:33). Most Christians have never put that promise to the test. From our files in The Peoples Church we could produce story after story of men and women who have made a promise to God in faith, often not knowing where the money was going to come from, and in a miraculous way God has sent it in.

We cannot finish the task with cash. The method is not cash but credit.

10

A "Five-Year Plan"

The famous "five-year plans" of Russia might be considered faith promises. Although he relied totally upon human resources and certainly did not know the system was biblical, Stalin purposed in his heart (II Corinthians 9:7) that he would transform one of the most backward states in the world into a great industrial power. To do this, after he had gained undisputed power in the U.S.S.R. by 1929 he innaugurated a series of five-year plans for the development of every aspect of growth in Russia.

He had managed to survive the chaotic struggle for power after Lenin's death in 1924, then faced the enormous task of unifying a still fragmented group of states and people. He turned a sprawling nation of serfs, or at best peasants, into a force to be reckoned with. Although aided by a series of ruthless purges that eliminated the opposition, most of this transition was a result of Stalin's five-year plans. It was a matter of breaking an impossibly gigantic project down into bite-sized pieces and determining what would be done during a certain time limit. Stalin might as well have filled in a faith promise envelope reading, "In dependence upon the character and determination of the peoples of the U.S.S.R. I will endeavor to do the following in a systematic way during the next five years."

After World War II China did the same thing with its sprawling, disintegrated and very individualistic peoples in a series of five-year plans, and Nehru was able to bring some order out of chaos in India when he adopted his first five-year plan in 1951.

My most recent encounter with this national "faith promise" system was in a visit to the Republic of Korea in 1979. There had been considerable unrest in South Korea immediately after the regime of the elderly Syngman Rhee who had become President in 1958. In a bloodless coup led by Major General Pak Chung Hi on July 3, 1961 the government once again began to stabilize and Pak (pronounced Park) was elected President on October 15,

1963. Since that time the development of the Republic of Korea may be one of the most dramatic phenomena of modern times.

I visited Korea five years after the Korean war (1950-1953). It was a sad sight, and I think almost anyone would have to admit that at that time (1958) Korea was standing in the world's breadline. The people were warm-hearted, attractive and very intelligent, but they had virtually nothing. Many of the relief agencies of the world were sending all sorts of aid and personnel. The United States government poured millions into South Korea during the post-war years.

I remember that there were almost no cars in Seoul, although British Land Rovers were very popular. They were apparently built with heavier steel and better able to withstand the impossible roads. Even in the capital city where there were a few miles of paved roads, it was a bit rough for a normal car and the country roads were out of the question for anything less sturdy than a jeep.

At that time there was only one fairly good hotel in the city of Seoul, The Bando, and there was very little industry. South Korea had always been the breadbasket of the country. Power sources and industry were all in the north. When the still uneasy truce of July 20, 1953 was signed the south was completely cut off from power sources. The "border" between South and North Korea is one of the only ones like it in the world. Panmunjom is in the de-militarized zone where there is the only communication that exists, but it is extremely formal and in no way serves to connect the two countries. Rail, road and telephone communication is non-existent. In my letters home in 1958 I wrote:

"Korea is a land of jeeps. Actually, a lot of them are not jeeps. Some are English Land Rovers and others are a Korean imitation of a jeep. Apart from in downtown Seoul a normal car would be useless in Korea. The American jeeps and British Land Rovers are four-wheel drive vehicles, and it is amazing how often you have to use both rear and front and your low gear position. The Korean jeeps are used primarily as taxis and stay on the city streets. In addition to the jeeps there are quite a few large trucks, some motorcycles, hundreds of bicycles, the city buses, and an occasional car. Most of the latter are owned by government officials, army personnel, or rich businessmen. There are less than a half dozen each of the larger American cars. So few that everyone knows exactly who owns them.

"Most of our traveling has been done in Land Rovers. These may put the American jeep out of business in Korea before long. They are much stronger and can stand the gaff of Korean roads and trails. The steel frames of the jeeps often break right in half and have to be welded together again. The British vehicles are made of heavier steel and almost everyone in Korea likes them better.

"Seoul is not a beautiful city. At night there are no street lights. Many buildings still bear the scars of war. The people are poor. There are many nice homes but thousands of hovels. In the refugee sections it is appalling. You wonder how they can go on living. They go on living because they cannot die. There are still lots of orphans. Some are war orphans. Others are simply abandoned because they are not wanted. Still others deliberately send their child to an orphanage because they know that there he will get an education and they cannot afford such a luxury."

When I returned to the Republic of Korea for the first time in 1979 I could not believe what I saw. It has been changed from a poor, rural community to an affluent, industrial nation within a short fifteen years. The city of Seoul is an almost continuous traffic jam. Most of the cars, like the "Pony," are built from scratch in Korea. There are skyscrapers on all sides. The hotel where I stayed, The Chosun, boasts twenty floors, and the newer Lotte towers forty stories high. These are just two of a large group of big "five-star" hotels.

The same situation exists throughout the Republic, and it has all come about as a result of a series of five-year plans in which the government determined or purposed to do certain things within a given period of time. How else does one face the baffling task of turning a rural society without power sources into the affluent, industrial force that it is today?

Part of the first plan was to connect Pusan in the south with Seoul in the north. When the highway was being built some thought it was unnecessary — especially when many of the people were still poor and often hungry. But the Pak government had a goal and this was one of the things that could be done during the early stages of development. Now it is an intrinsic part of Korea's economy. In the beginning it was just one year's installment on a five-year faith promise. A year's payment didn't amount to much, but the final results have been mind-boggling.

Business

This same faith promise system is used in most large business enterprises. Business planning meetings often gather around things called long-range goals and short-range goals. Usually the long-range goals seem to be out of the question. They are simply too big for us. It is difficult to visualize them and they are so far distant that they discourage us. It is only when these huge long-range objectives can be broken down into a series of short-range objectives that the average person can grasp them and not be discouraged.

Finances

Most of us have used the same system in our financial planning. An insurance policy is a sort of faith promise. We purpose over a period of years to pay what seems like a small amount into a policy that will accumulate to what may be a large amount at the end of twenty years.

Buildings

Shortly after we made a major move to a new location of The Peoples Church we envisioned an additional complex of educational facilities that would cost a total of approximately two million dollars. The cost was so high for us at that time and the buildings so complex that I don't think any of us could have tackled the task. However, our architect was able to break it down into five phases that could be built over a period of time and at a price for each phase that was within our reach.

We have now completed all but a third floor on our highschool building and have paid for a total of four segments of a rather complex Christian education structure that is now in full use. It was the faith promise principle that made it possible. My only regret is that we did not do a more comprehensive planning job twenty years ago. It would have saved a lot of headaches in the process of tearing down and rebuilding.

This is just another way of explaining some aspects of a faith promise offering. It involves planning. As an individual the task baffles me. Even a share in the support of one missionary is too big. Any other good-sized missionary project seems out of sight for me. Unless — unless I do for missions what I may have done in other areas. I promise a relatively small amount month by month for the following year.

What have I done? I have launched my own five-year plan. I have taken the first step toward my long-range goal. I have committed myself to an insurance policy. I've broken down my building complex into phases. Only the cause is not a nation, a firm, a personal benefit, or even a church complex. The cause is the ultimate evangelization of a world. And my resources are not merely the mobilization of human ability, but the unlimited potential of my faith and the untapped reservoirs of the power of God.

11

Let's Admit the Bottleneck

Missionary work involves two groups of people, the goers and the senders. The Bible makes this quite clear. "How shall they preach, except they be sent?" (Romans 10:15). To suggest that everyone ought to be a missionary on the foreign field is just as foolish as to say everyone should be in the army and sent overseas during a war. Every nation realizes that it takes two kinds of people to wage a successful war. There must be the manpower on the firing line, but there must also be those who are able to send him there, keep him there, and supply him with ammunition. It usually takes scores of people at home for every one that is at the front.

So it is with the war of world evangelization. The soldier of the cross on the mission field cannot operate without the soldier of the cross in the business office and in the home. Even the apostle Paul had to be sent by the church at Antioch and supported by many of the other churches in order to carry on his missionary work. God does not give everybody the privilege of working in the front lines of the battle. Some are called to maintain the supply lines at home where there is not much glamor or glitter or glory or adventure.

The problem that confronts us is this: the task is not finished. Millions of people have not yet seen their first missionary. Where is the bottleneck? Do we lack personnel or do we lack money?

We lack money. The people are available. Never has there been a generation when there were so many well-trained young people anxious to do the will of God. Our Bible schools and Christian colleges in North America alone are turning them out every year by the hundreds, and a poll of almost every evangelical school will reveal that a good percentage of these young people would be willing to go to the mission field. The sad truth of the matter is that only a very small percentage of them actually go. Briercrest Bible Institute and Prairie Bible Institute in Canada have about the highest percentage of their graduates on the mission field, and that amounts to only twenty percent or less.

Where is the breakdown? Why is it that more young people who want to go to the field do not get there? Let me give you the answer with a personal illustration. In 1951 some of the Youth for Christ leaders came back from the Orient to a conference at Winona Lake, Indiana. I shall never forget that year. The doors in Formosa and Japan were wide open. The men from these places spoke many times, and always their plea was the same: "We need men for the Orient. I have come home to find men."

That year they found the men — not just a few, but hundreds of them, young people whose hearts were moved by the appeals. I saw them as they made their way forward in the Billy Sunday Tabernacle indicating their desire to go. I was one of them. The Rev. John Henderson was another. We had been holding evangelistic campaigns throughout Canada and the United States for several years, treading on the toes of others who were doing exactly the same thing. At that time we were not really needed at home. Here was an opportunity to go where we were needed desperately.

Since the appeal had been made particularly for teams that included a preacher and a person with some kind of musical ability, my song leader and I constituted exactly what they wanted. We applied, and were accepted by the Council of Youth for Christ International to go to the Philippines. What a thrill it was!

To this day neither John Henderson nor I have set foot on the Philippine Islands as missionaries. Why? Youth for Christ asked us to do what any missionary society must ask — raise the money for your fares and your salaries, and we will send you. I did not know how to raise the money, and it was an enormous amount, much more than the average missionary had to raise to go to the field. My father had made it a policy not to do anything special financially for his own family that he could not do for others. Thus what The Peoples Church could have done would have been only a drop in the bucket.

We were just two young men amongst hundreds of others, most of whom to this day have not left the shores of America. In this case the bottleneck was certainly not men. It was money.

For seven years I was the associate pastor of The Peoples Church, and since January, 1959 I have been the pastor. Our office is in contact with the mission field every day. Almost every week we receive a letter from one of the faith missions that reads something like this: "We have three young people who are accepted candidates for the mission field. Can you help us with their support?" Or like this: "We have a young couple who are urgently needed on the field. We lack their personal support. Could your people help us?"

Sometimes we are able to answer in the affirmative, but in the majority of cases we have to refuse. So far our people have only supplied enough funds to share in the support of about five hundred missionaries and nationals. Gradually we are trying to increase that number, but we have almost reached the saturation point of giving in The Peoples Church.

What does this mean? Simply that almost every faith missionary society, and some of the denominational missionary societies, have accepted candidates still at home because they do not have sufficient funds to send them to the field. Hold a missionary convention, and you will find that most organizations can send a half dozen new recruits to appeal to the people every year.

Have you ever noticed the number of young people who are going about the country doing deputational work? There is a steady stream of them at our prayer meetings, our young people's organizations, our Sunday Schools, and other church gatherings. What are they doing? They are trying to raise their support, hoping and praying that some businessperson, some Bible class, some church will say, "We'll send you to the field." And most of them waste six months, a year, and in some cases several years waiting for God's people at home to be sufficiently stirred to send them. I say "waste" even though I know that there are fringe benefits that accrue during a young person's deputational work — experience, testing, learning to live by faith, etc. It is my opinion that to get them on the field as soon as possible far outweighs the advantages of a tour to raise their support. This is one asset of applying to a denominational board. If one is accepted, the denomination usually assumes the responsibility of support. Certainly, some deputational work may be required — but not the formidable task of raising the large amount that is needed for the support of modern foreign missionaries.

Obviously, the breakdown is not men. It is money. We have the people. Every church sees them as they pass through month after month, and the main reason we see them is that we have not supplied the money.

In my evangelistic work throughout the world I usually set aside a night to preach on missions. At the close of the service I extend an invitation in these words: "How many young people thirty years of age and under, will say: If God wants me to be a missionary, I will be one. Come forward and stand at the front of the auditorium." I have done this all over the world and almost inevitably every Christian young person in the building will stand up, come forward, and declare: "If God makes it clear to me that He wants me to be a missionary, I'll be a missionary."

Suppose I were to make an appeal for funds to the business and professional people in the same audience in these words: "How many will stand up and say: If God wants me to give Him fifty percent of my income for foreign missions, I will do it." What sort of response would I get? One, half a dozen, or a score of people out of an audience of two thousand? More than likely there would be no response whatsoever. We expect our young people to lay down their lives for God, but most of us are not willing to lay down our bank accounts.

We have the men, but we do not have the money. If we had the money, we could get the task completed in our generation. This is the bottleneck of world evangelization.

Someone may become alarmed because I seem to be saying that we no longer need volunteers. We have more than we can use. Not at all! I spend a lot of time asking for personnel. Others devote a great deal more time than I to the task of recruiting people. We never seem to have enough.

The last time I talked to Dr. Phillip Butler, founder of "Intercristo," an organization that catalogs Christian job opportunities around the world, he told me that he could produce seventeen thousand requests for personnel — the majority missionary in nature.

This is just one society. Many of the missions have extensive lists of their personnel needs that may not be cataloged by Intercristo. "World Vision, International" usually keeps a long list of Christian missionary job opportunities. Can you imagine how many requests for people could be accumulated if we were to put all of these lists in one place?

Of course, there is a constant urgent need for people, but even after we get the people they still must go through the bottleneck of money in most cases, and some of them just can't make it.

People we need, but the bottleneck is money.

12

Christian Priorities

The meaning of the word "charity" is love, but in our time it seems to have changed so that it applies primarily to things that have to do with relief work. When we think of charity we usually see rescue missions, bread lines, soup kitchens and handouts of some kind, and too often "charity" is given from our leftovers.

In this sense, for nearly two thousand years we have been giving God our charity. We give Him charity when it comes to prayer. Most Christians decide on their prayer time by checking their day's activities, marking off the periods that are taken up with important things, and giving God what is left over. Instead of setting aside the best time of the day for God, we have given Him charity. Prayer time is the period that is no good for anything else.

During the special missions that come to our city or town we give God our charity. We think of all the things we must do each night of the week, and whatever night is left over we go to the mission. In this generation seldom does a Christian anticipate the special mission and then deliberately block off those nights on the calendar for God, eliminate all less important projects and give God the entire week. Oh, what a blessing there could be in your town if a few hundred Christians and their families would give a week or two to God for evangelism. Yet when it comes to local evangelism we give God what is left over — charity.

The Old Piano

Occasionally in our church office the telephone will ring and the voice of some good Christian person will say: "We are in the process of buying a new grand piano for our home, and I wonder if you could use our old one in the church?" Of course, we never say no. We have old pianos all over the church, and we are very grateful for them; but I have yet to hear a voice at the other end of the telephone line say, "We are about to buy a new grand piano for our home, but we have decided that the old upright will do for us. Could we make a gift to the church of the new grand?"

The Indian Baby

The young man had just arrived in India. He was walking along the banks of the Ganges. He passed an Indian woman. In her arms was a fat, healthy baby girl. By the hand she was holding an anaemic little boy. It was obvious that he would not live very long. His body was contorted by disease. The young missionary looked and passed by. An hour later he returned. There stood the same woman. The frail little boy was still there, but the fat healthy baby girl was gone.

The young man spoke, "I saw you here a short time ago and there were two children. One was a very fine baby girl. What happened to her?"

"I threw her into the Ganges. It is a part of my religion."

"But if you were forced to sacrifice one of your children why did you not keep the healthy child and throw the disease-ridden boy into the Ganges? He would not have lived long at best."

The heathen woman drew herself up proudly, and before she turned to walk away with the dying boy, she said with a note of fervor in her voice, "Sir, in our country when we give our god something, we always give him the best we have."

The Haitian Church

When I was in Haiti in 1949 I had the privilege of preaching to the Haitian Christians at the annual Christians' Convention of the World Team Mission. I spoke several times each day to audiences of over six thousand people. I shall never forget them. They had a prayer meeting every morning at six o'clock. Two thousand of them came to pray.

They had come to the convention in many different ways. Some had ridden long distances on their little donkeys. Some had come by commione, or Haitian bus. When they load a bus in Haiti, it is filled to overflowing! I took pictures of some of the buses as they arrived. There were people inside, on the top, hanging on both sides, and some were walking ahead and others behind. They arrived singing gospel hymns in their own language. Most of the people walked to the meetings. I met a number who had walked through the valleys and over the hills for more than fifty miles, and after the convention they walked home again.

While they were there the women slept on the benches in the tabernacle. The men slept out on the ground. They cooked their meals over small fires built on the hard sunbaked dirt of the fields.

At the close of the conference the missionaries took a survey of their offerings for the past year. The average Haitian farmer in that district makes about eighty-five to a hundred American dollars a year. That is all the cash these people ever see. When the survey was made, to my amazement I learned that they had given over ten thousand American dollars for the support of their own churches and for world evangelization. That year some of their money was sent as a missionary gift to one of the American Bible societies.

I was put to shame as I was confronted with the sacrificial giving of these people who had lived in the darkness of voodooism only a few years before. Nowhere in the Christian countries had I ever seen such giving. Where did they learn it? They learned it in their heathenism. Pagan religions demand the best of their followers. They are not content with charity. They must have the choice, and they get it.

For generations we have been trying to do the work of spreading the gospel around the world with the charity of Christians. The majority of our missionary work has been carried on with the leftovers of God's people. Old pianos, old medical instruments, old clothes, old books, old cars and old money — money that we have decided can be of no legitimate use to us.

This is not intended to disparage or take lightly the contribution of used or old articles to the mission field. This is a work that needs to be done and it takes a lot of organization and effort. But as I think of these things I remember the words of our Lord when He was talking about tithes and offerings in relation to the heavy injunctions of the Law of Moses: "These ought ye to have done and not to leave the others undone" (Matthew 23:23).

What a transformation there would be if once in a while we would keep the charity for ourselves and give God the choice!

Let's Talk About Sacrifice

In an earlier section we discussed the question of sacrifice. In other words, how much is it hurting any of us because we give largely to God? Suppose some do see our responsibility to God as far as giving is concerned, and make a contribution that costs something. Have they really sacrificed? Have they suffered privation either on the going end or the giving end?

Certainly God does not need people? He could have done the work alone, or He would not be God. God does not need you in the foreign field to help Him with His work. God does not need my little bit of money to help Him carry out His purpose. He owns the cattle on a thousand hills and the diamonds in a hundred mines. The glory of the gospel is not that God needs us, but that in His love and graciousness He has given us the privilege of working with Him. "For we are labourers together with God" (I Corinthians 3:9).

If Queen Elizabeth II were to dispatch a message to me to the effect that she would like me to leave my home and friends and come over to Great Britain to help her with some project, what would my reaction be? Would I count the cost carefully, consider the sacrifice involved, and rather reluctantly answer in the affirmative? No. Without a moment's hesitation, I would board the plane to London and get on with the job. Most British citizens would deem it a privilege to work with the Queen.

The Queen will never give me the privilege of helping her with a project, but the thing that humbles me is the fact that the King of kings has enlisted my help in the greatest project in the world. He tells me I can go. I can pray. I can give my money. It would almost be blasphemous to think of it as a privation. Working with God is not a privation but a privilege.

13

We Will Now Receive The Offering

Schools do not teach us some of the things we need to know. This is true when we train for any sort of career. The schools we attend do everything they can do in most cases to prepare their students for their chosen careers, but there are many things that seem to be ignored in the classroom and others that can be learned nowhere else but in the field of experience. Some schools are a lot better than others when it comes to practical training and some are almost totally "ivory tower" in their approach.

At the practical level the primary task of any educational institution is two-fold: first, to teach its students how to study, and second, to show them how to find the materials and information they may need when they start working. An institution that accomplishes these is fulfilling its essential role and has every reason to exist.

However, in my opinion, almost every school could improve its practical training and be a little more realistic in telling students the "facts of life" in their profession, business, trade or whatever. Granted, there are areas of every career that cannot be taught. They must be experienced, but there are also other things that are known and could be taught.

In any area of the Lord's work one of the topics schools seem to back away from is the actual mechanics of how to take an offering and how to raise money in other ways. I suppose this is a result of the age-old vacant room in the mind of many church people — that makes them think there is something wrong about asking for financial support and that it would be a great thing if we could operate the Lord's work without ever taking an offering. In this sort of mind, then, money for God's work is not a very spiritual thing, and so, in many areas long hours over many years are spent training young people how to study the Bible, how to teach it, how to organize Sunday Schools, how to develop curricula for them, how to conduct music, arrange music, sing or play instruments — with very little attention paid to the fact that none of these other abilities are of much value unless there is a place to do them, people to listen, and an organization to carry forth our ministries.

The young ministers, musicians, or missionaries are not out of school very long before they learn how important the ability to finance their work really is, and how limited their spiritual service will be if they cannot pay their bills.

There are physical activities connected with most of our Christian service. We must learn how to put the elements on a communion table and know the general procedure about how this ordinance may be conducted, before we can be blessed by the spiritual benefits of the Lord's supper.

Before we preach someone puts chairs on a platform, lights in a pulpit and maybe turns on a public address system. These are necessary and they are spiritual.

The musician learns where to place the sections of the choir, how to arrange the music it will sing, the logistics of getting people from the choir room to the choir loft decently and in order. All of this, before anyone can sing the praise of God effectively.

The ultimate goal of the Christian educational director is to teach people the Word of God and prepare them for service, but these important "spiritual" things cannot be done until the rooms have been set up, blackboards have been cleared, rolls have been taken, etc. It would be a mistake to say that the teaching is spiritual and the logistics of the set-up and organization are not.

By the time you have read this far you know that I think of the giving of God's people as an extremely spiritual matter, because that is the way the Bible treats it. Remember, it is one of the graces of the Christian life. But seldom does anyone explain the logistics of asking for an offering.

Any Sort of Offering

We should never apologize for the offering. If you feel that you must apologize, you had better not take it at all.

People will generally respond better when they are happy, but in most cases an "offering joke" does not help much. You should choose a time in the service when the people are rejoicing in the blessings of God. Occasionally, a sad or solemn atmosphere may result in a great response, but this is the exception rather than the rule. Happy people give more generously than sad people.

Do not put pressure on people all the time. All of us become immune to this kind of pressure rather quickly and we arm ourselves against it. Very rarely should it be necessary to take two offerings in one service. Sometimes this can be effective, but usually only if some new or unexpected cause has been presented and it is obvious that the people would like an opportunity of contributing to it. There are many services in The Peoples Church when I call for the ushers as simply as possible and mention no special cause whatsoever. Then, when there is a real need the people will listen and respond. Every service or program should not be a sort of financial crisis.

The three major methods that may be used (although there are probably many others) are:

- Take a retiring offering. Have ushers, or an offering box, at the door for the convenience of people as they leave the service. This would be the way that the smallest offering possible would be given.
- Pass the plates. This is by far the most commonly used method. Except under rare circumstances this produces much more than a retiring offering.
- Use envelopes. A general rule of thumb would be that offering envelopes will about double the amount that is given if envelopes are not used. Envelopes lend an importance to the offering that is usually not achieved if it is just taken in the natural course of events.

These are the main methods, but any method is improved by a great cause. There should be frequent services in which the offering is received for some particular need. Our people are intelligent and they are a bit reluctant to give very largely to general causes or for rather evasive uses. We need to confront our folk with a great deal of respect for their intelligence, and whenever possible state the facts of the need. It doesn't have to be on a highly emotional level. Sometimes it is enough to say: "Here is what we have. This is what we need. Now is our opportunity to take care of it."

A Faith Promise Offering

I have already said a great deal about the biblical basis, the essential principles and the philosophy of a faith promise offering. Now, I will deal with the logistics. How do you do it?

What is the mechanical procedure of actually putting this good scriptural method into operation?

In every department of our Sunday School we receive a faith promise offering each Sunday morning during our World Missions Conference. We ask for a similar offering in all the sanctuary services, both morning and night, of each Sunday. Because our conference involves two weeks, this means that we repeat the faith promise offering for three consecutive Sundays.

Even if your conference only includes one Sunday you should take the offering on at least two. There are very few churches that have all of their people — even the dedicated ones — present on any single Sunday. In a large church it would usually take at least two or three Sundays to see all the faithful members. This is why most churches have a much larger number of members — even active ones — than they have seating capacity or attendance. If you take your faith promise offering only on one Sunday you will miss many of your people. This is true of any equally important offering.

Every year I prepare a printed outline describing how leaders should ask for faith promises in their classes or departments of our Sunday School. Then I talk to them at a Sunday School workers' meeting and very carefully explain each step. They may vary it from class to class, but it gives them something to start with — based on the success of more than fifty conferences in our own church, as well as scores of others all over the world in just about every denomination and kind of church. These have been conferences where I was usually the main speaker and often responsible for taking the offering.

- *Explain your objectives.* In any faith promise offering the people must know how the church expects to use the money. I usually tell my people how much we need in order to maintain our existing commitments. I outline these in broad terms — how many missionaries we are helping and at what cost, also what projects we are already involved in. Our home missions projects are also outlined. People want to know how much of their money will go to foreign countries and how much will be used at home for things like rescue missions, Bible schools, and missions whose work is primarily at home. We try to keep by far the majority of our resources for missions going to foreign fields of the world, but very few object if some of it is used for good projects at home.

If you are a large church and your missionary income is quite high, you will discover that eventually you may have to use a percentage of it for overhead. In 1978 we used approximately eleven percent for overhead — that is, to share the cost of utilities, maintenance, salaries, office supplies, etc., without which the missionary department could not function, and if it did not function there would be no missions income whatever. When our faith promise was small we were able to use it all for missions and the local church budget carried the overhead, which was also small.

When I announce the amount we need to maintain existing commitments I often say "We need 'X' thousands of dollars just to stand still."

- *Give out the envelopes.* Although we have already sent envelopes and an appeal letter to all of our people, we never depend on that, nor do we rely on having envelopes in the pews. We have the ushers come down the aisles and give enough envelopes to the person at the end of the pew so that there is more than enough for everyone — including husbands, wives and children.

Avoid having the ushers count the envelopes so that there is exactly one for each person. That takes too long. You can afford to be liberal with the envelopes. You will need four or five times the number of envelopes than the number that will be used. Some of those that are left over can be picked up after the service.

Don't ask the people who want one to put up their hands and ask for one as the ushers go up the aisles. Most of them won't do it. One of the secrets of good participation in a faith promise offering is to get an envelope into the hands of everyone in the building. I usually say, "Would you be courteous enough to take one. I want everyone to have one when we read it together. Wives, don't let your husbands do all the giving for the family. Be sure every child receives one. The only way people will ever learn how to give is by developing the habit from childhood. Even if you have already filled out one envelope in another service, take another. Give God a chance to speak to you again. You may want to turn in a second envelope that adds to your earlier promise."

You see, as the conference goes on, more information is given out, a better vision of the fields has been received and God will often speak very definitely to people and urge them to do more than they have already done. Be sure they have an envelope in their hands so that they can obey God if He should speak to them.

If you really trust God yourself, then you should be expecting Him to work all the time. Giving out envelopes is an indication of the preacher's faith. He is getting prepared for God to work among his people.

- *Read what the envelope says.* Ask your people to follow you from their envelope as you read. Generally it reads something like this: "In dependence upon God I will endeavor to give the amount checked month by month for the next twelve months toward the World Missions program of this church."

The main words to emphasize are "in dependence upon God." Point out that this is a promise that is contingent on God's supply. "I will endeavor" means that you will give it if God provides it. All you are doing now is committing it to God before you have it. Then when it comes there will be no question about how it will be used. Your faith promise has already decided that. If there should be some unforeseen reversal in your circumstances, you are not stuck with a pledge you cannot keep. If you don't receive it, you can't give it.

- *Explain the Faith Promise System.* You can never do this too often. Some new people have never heard about it — others have heard but haven't learned. There are still others who have learned and haven't responded.

It has been my privilege to help with the conference and offering of the First Presbyterian Church of Jackson, Mississippi, over a period of a dozen consecutive years. During the early years Dr. John Reed Miller was minister and when he retired Dr. Donald Patterson was gracious enough to continue asking me back. Both of these pastors have contributed substantially to the spirit of World Missions that pervades many of the Presbyterian churches in the deep South.

After a few years with Dr. Miller he used to draw me aside before each Sunday service and urge me to explain the faith promise again. As a result, every year there were people who made a promise in this way for the first time. Even after fifty years of explanation in The Peoples Church we still have some folk who never made a faith promise.

The points to cover in your own way are:

a) This is not a cash offering. You don't need cash to participate. Having explained this, I usually add that we are using an envelope, so that if some wish to put in their first installment, they can do so. If visitors wish to make a one-time cash offering, they can do so. You will lose a considerable potential for missions if you use a card rather than an envelope. Our envelopes also have a flap that is a blank check form already made out to The Peoples Church. Although they will sometimes protest, most banks will accept a blank check form if it is properly filled out. In many places banks are required to do this despite their computer markings. Available check forms always increase an offering.

But then quickly return to the concept that this is not a cash offering.

b) Emphasize that it is not a pledge in the sense that no one will ever ask them for it. It is a covenant between a person and God. It is turned in to the church so that an intelligent budget can be drawn up by the missionary committee for the next twelve months — based on the faith of the people.

c) It is a faith promise. At this point I generally quote the basic verse, "Every man (every woman, every boy, every girl) as he purposeth in his heart, so let him give" (II Corinthians 9:7). Sometimes this verse is on the envelope and you can read it.

d) Describe the difference between an intelligent promise and a foolish one. I have dealt with this at great length in my exposition of Corinthians, chapter eight. Now, in brief I usually say, "It would be foolish to promise one dollar more than the Holy Spirit is urging upon you. It would be just as foolish to promise less. Listen to the voice of God, and as you pray about what you should do, God will direct you."

- *Pray with the people about the amount they should give.* For many it will be the first time they have ever done this. They will need good sense and divine guidance.
- *Give the people time to fill in their envelopes.* Generally, it is better to avoid filling in this time with anything else that might distract them from their faith promise. Sometimes, I continue talking a little bit about the offering. Often, I just stop, and ask the organist to play some background music. I don't move out of the pulpit. I just stand there and wait until it is obvious that people have finished writing and are ready to turn in their envelopes.
- *Collect the promises.* We usually have the ushers come forward and pass the plates and then carry them to the office where we have a trained staff to tabulate the total. When I was

young my father used to have the promises brought to a table where the monthly gift was multiplied by twelve. Then someone brought them to the pulpit and he would read out the yearly amounts — without names, of course. From there the envelopes were taken to workers with adding machines who gave him totals from time to time until the final amount was in.

This used to be a rather exciting kind of offering — sometimes a bit noisy, but in those early days it did a lot to make people "faith promise" conscious. I preach at some conferences that still do this, and very often the results are good. Usually they are churches where my father led their first conference and taught them how to do it by calling out amounts and using adding machines.

More than ten years ago I decided to take a chance and just collect the envelopes and have them tabulated in the office. While this is going on we have the main speaker preach. Once the offering is over he can concentrate on some other aspect of world missions. By the time he is finished, the office has sent me the total. I announce it and have the congregation sing the doxology. On the final Sunday night, after the grand total has been announced we have the choir sing *The Hallelujah Chorus*. It can be a service to the glory of God that few people ever forget.

14

How Can We Hear God Speak?

How Can We Hear God Speak? was the topic of my sermon, preached on February 2, 1967 at the Moody Founder's Week conference. It was transcribed, edited to some extent and published by the Moody Bible Institute in their "Founder's Week Messages." I have revised it further, but it still differs in style from the other chapters of this book because it reflects to some extent my preaching before a live audience as opposed to my writing at a desk.

****

I want to talk to you a bit about how you and I can hear the voice of God in 1967.

When I was about thirteen years of age, I sat in a meeting something like this. The speaker was a missionary. I have forgotten a great deal of what he said, but I do remember this. Somewhere in the middle of his message he said there was a time as a young man when he heard the voice of God calling him to be a missionary in Africa. He responded to that voice and gave his life to God. Now he had spent twenty-five years ministering the Word of God in the land of Africa.

I sat back in the pew and was stirred. I thought what a wonderful thing that was, what an exciting experience that must be, actually to hear the voice of God; to be conscious that God is speaking to you, that He is telling you what to do, how to do it, when to do it, where to do it, and to know that you're moving out in response to the direct command of the voice of God. Then, I remember, I hung my head as I thought back over my thirteen years, most of which I had spent in the confines of a wonderful, evangelical, spiritual church. I said to myself, "Paul Smith, you have heard a great many voices in your lifetime. You've heard the voice of your mother, the voice of your father, the voice of your Sunday school teacher. You've heard the voice of the minister. You've heard the voices of your neighbors. You've lived all these thirteen years and God has never said a thing to you." I concluded there was something wrong.

A year or two went by and I came to another service. This time it was an evangelistic crusade. Again I forget a great deal of what the evangelist said, but I do remember in the course of his message he gave a little excerpt of his own personal testimony. He talked first of all of how God found him and saved him. Then he described a scene in which he was walking down a country road, and after painting a very vivid picture, he said, "And that day, I heard the voice of God, and God called me to be an evangelist. I gave my life to the evangelistic ministry and now for the past thirty-five years I have been conducting evangelistic campaigns around the world."

I don't think I heard much of the rest of his message because I was thinking. I was thinking how wonderful, how exciting, what a terrific thing it must be to remember the time and place so that you can describe the circumstances when you actually heard God's voice and knew that this was the way, and that God had said, "Walk in it." I remember again I hung my head a little bit, for by now I had attended a great many more services, had read my Bible a great deal more, had lived a relatively good Christian life; yet up until that time, for fifteen years in fact while apparently other people on every side of me, missionaries, pastors, evangelists, teachers, had heard the voice of God — I had not heard a thing. I thought there must be something wrong with me.

Since those days, I have learned some facts about how God speaks to people that I did not know when I was fifteen years of age, and I would like to outline for you five ways in which God speaks. I know as I look over this great congregation there are young people, middle-aged people, older people who are still asking themselves the questions, "What does God want me to do? Where does God want me to go?" Some of you have come to this conference hoping that at some time in one of these services you will at least hear the voice of God and be able to say, "This is it," and forever after be able to remember this 1967 Moody Founder's Week as the time you heard God speak to you.

Perhaps Audibly

Now, if you hear God during these days, *how* will you hear Him? Some of you more conservative people may object to my first point, but it happens to be in the Bible, and I believe in preaching everything in the Bible whether people object to it or not. There is no way that you can read the Word of God without coming to the conclusion that the voice of God may be heard audibly. Again and again the Bible says God spoke to a man, to a woman, to a group of people.

Adam and Eve heard the voice of God. You remember it occurs in Genesis. They were walking in the garden in the cool of the day, and the Bible says they heard the voice of God. It does not say they read a book. It does not say they had a vision. It does not say they experienced a dream. It does not say they had a strong impression. It does not say somebody else brought a message to them. It does not introduce an angel. It simply says they heard the voice of God. The Bible doesn't explain it, it just states it.

Elijah heard the voice of God. You remember Elijah was right at the pinnacle of his success as a prophet and preacher. He had gone through that dramatic experience on top of Mount Carmel when he had called down the fire of God to consume his sacrifice. He had gone through that experience in a land that had had three years of drought; and as he had prayed seven times on the mountain, the rain had come down in a deluge. You talk about success. You talk about blessing. You talk about inspiration. You talk about victory. This man Elijah was at the top as far as success was concerned. Then suddenly he became the most discouraged man in the country.

It is worthwhile noticing that very often our greatest periods of discouragement and despondency follow our greatest spiritual experiences and success. Often when a businessman has put through the best deal of his career, the next day he will have an emotional slump. Have you ever made the mistake of attempting to telephone your minister on Monday morning? Don't ever do it. A minister perhaps experiences the great blessing of God in the house of God on Sunday, and I suppose there is nothing quite comparable to the joy of opening the Word of God and expounding it with all its promises and inspiration, all its commands, to a waiting congregation, and then, seeing men and women respond to the invitation to accept Jesus Christ as Savior. There's nothing quite as thrilling as that. Possibly the most difficult part of it is to live through Monday when it's all over for a little while.

This was Elijah's problem. He had had everything there was for a prophet to have, and then he became discouraged and scared, and he ran. He ran and found a cave in which to hide. There he sat down and felt sorry for himself. He thought, "Here am I, the great prophet of God, and I'm the only one left that still believes God. Poor me!" Every once in a while I meet a minister like that, who thinks he is the only person in town who still believes the Bible. Bless your heart, you're never the only one left. God never leaves Himself with only one person.

If any man needed to hear from God right then, it was Elijah. He wanted to know what the next move was. As he sat there feeling sorry for himself, outside he heard the blast of a great wind. Elijah quickly got up, went to the mouth of the cave, looked out, and watched that wind as it swept across the ground. He was thinking, "Now in this wind, certainly in this unusual phenomenon, God is going to tell me something. I'll watch it, I'll wait, and out of the wind I'll hear the voice of God." But Elijah waited in vain. Finally the wind blew itself out and died down. There wasn't a voice.

Elijah went back into the cave and sat down to continue nursing his sorrow. As he sat there, he felt the ground under him tilting a little bit. He thought, "Why there's hardly ever an earthquake in these parts, but I believe I'm sitting here in the middle of an earthquake." He went to the mouth of the cave again, and sure enough, the ground in front of him was rolling perceptibly, almost like the sea. Elijah said, "This is it. God is going to speak to me through this unusual phenomenon." He watched, and waited with baited breath, and eventually the earthquake stopped; and there hadn't been a word from God.

He was just about to turn around and go back into the cave when he noticed a little bush burning. Elijah said, "Ah, this is it. God is going to speak to me the way He spoke to Moses." Elijah waited and watched, and eventually the fire burned the bush down completely and went out. God hadn't said a thing.

Then the Bible says that after the wind, after the earthquake, after the fire, there was a still, small voice" (I Kings 19:9-12). Elijah heard the voice of God audibly.

You can go through your Bible until you get to the book of Revelation and there John on the Isle of Patmos heard the voice of God that sounded like a trumpet.

So I cannot help concluding on the basis of the teaching of the Word of God that the voice of God may be heard audibly. Some folk interpret the last part of the thirteenth chapter of First

Corinthians in such a way that they get rid of any possibility of anyone in our times actually hearing the voice of God. They feel that all revelation ended toward the end of the apostles' lives. Frankly, on the basis of historical evidence, I am inclined to agree with them, but I cannot prove it by Scripture. Certainly, no scholarly exposition of these verses in Corinthians would lead us to believe that God would never talk audibly to people after the Bible was completed.

If I were to ask how many in this congregation have heard the voice of God, I know some would say, "Mr. Smith, I know exactly what you're talking about. There was a time and a place and a situation when I actually heard the voice of God." However, I also know that if I were to ask for a show of hands, there would be many people who would raise their hands with me and say, "As far as I can remember in my experience, I have never heard the voice of God audibly." I would have to say that. God has never said a word to me audibly. Before I go on may I suggest that if there has been a time in your life when you have heard the voice of God audibly, this does not give you the right to think or say that there is something wrong with me when I say that I have not. Because I have lived for nearly sixty years and have never heard the voice of God audibly at any time it does not give me the right to look at you and say, "Neither have you." Let's simply leave it where the Bible leaves it. The voice of God may be heard audibly.

Frequently — Through Signs

Frequently the voice of God is heard through signs. The outstanding example of this in the Old Testament is the story of Gideon. Gideon had the impression that he should be the leader of his people, that in some way God was calling him to serve. But Gideon thought what a terrible thing it would be if he should assume leadership and it really wasn't of God. If he could only be sure that this was in reality the voice of God speaking to him, then he could go ahead with confidence. You remember Gideon said, "I'm going to make a test. I'm going to put a little bit of wool out on the threshing floor tonight. If in the morning the wool is wet with dew but the ground around it is absolutely dry, then I will know that God wants me to be the leader of this people." So Gideon did that. The next morning he opened the back door, walked out, and every step he took a little cloud of dust rose up from his heels. You talk about dry ground, it was as dry as the desert sand. He reached down and picked up that bit of wool and it was soaking wet.

Gideon went back into his house with the little bit of wet wool and said, "This is it. God really . . . Oh, wait a minute. Maybe that was just a coincidence. I'll reverse it. This time I'll put the wool out and if in the morning the ground is wet and the wool is dry, then I will know absolutely that this is the voice of God and I am to be the leader of the people." So Gideon did that. The next morning when he opened the door and was about to step out, he had to stop and go back for his rubber boots. You talk about dew. He splashed his way across the threshing floor, reached down, picked up the bit of wool and it was bone dry.

Suppose you could have cornered Gideon when he was an old man and asked "Gideon, how did you know you were supposed to be the leader of your people? How did you hear the voice of God?" Do you know what he probably would have said? "Many years ago when I was still a young man, one day I heard the voice of God calling me to be the leader of this people. I responded and God was with me." But in reality, at that time Gideon did not hear a word audibly. He heard the voice of God through a sign.

Sometimes — Other People

Sometimes the voice of God is heard through other people. A classic story in the Bible about this concerns David. He became the second king of Israel. Do you remember how David knew he was to be king? God spoke to a man, a prophet, a judge by the name of Samuel. God said, "Samuel, there is a young man whom I want you to anoint to be the next king of my people. He lives in the home of Jesse." You will recall that exciting story of how Samuel went to Jesse's home, looked over all the sons, and finally, when David came in, he anointed him to be the king. David became the greatest king the Jewish people ever had.

If you were to have talked to David when he was an old man, after the battles and the rebellions were over, the nation had been established and he had settled the kingdom for the reign of his son, Solomon, you might have asked; "How did it happen that you knew you were to be the next king?" I think old King David would have smiled and said, "When I was a boy on my father's farm herding sheep, one day I heard the voice of God calling me to be king. I responded, and God was with me." But the facts of history are that at that time David heard no sound, no voice. God spoke to a prophet and the prophet spoke to David.

More than sixty years ago now, in a small village about one hundred miles from Toronto, a farmer's daughter organized a Sunday School class in the little brick schoolhouse at Cody's Corners. The farmer's sons and some of the workmen's sons used to come on Sunday afternoon. It was the only church they had. There was a Presbyterian church that was served infrequently whenever the preacher could come. One Sunday afternoon she was sitting there surrounded by ten or eleven boys, and before she taught the lesson she was moved by the Spirit of God to say, "Do you know, any one of you boys might be a minister." On her left hand side was an anaemic, thin, poorly-clad country boy who looked as if he wasn't going to last for many years. He sat there and listened, and without saying a word he responded in his heart, "God helping me, I am going to be that boy."

God took that boy and sent him around the world many times preaching the gospel. God let that country boy write thirty-five books with a circulation of over seven million copies in one hundred and twenty-eight different languages. God let that country boy write one thousand, two hundred lyrics for gospel songs and hymns. God let that country boy establish a church in which he was able to preach to two thousand people every Sunday morning and two thousand people every Sunday night for more than thirty years, and lead them in a program in which that church has now given fourteen million dollars for world missions.

That country boy is my dad. Today he is eighty-nine years of age. If you were to sit down with my father and ask him to reminisce about the early days, he'd be delighted to do so, and he would say something like this: "Do you know, when I was a fourteen-year-old boy, one day I heard the voice of God calling me to be a minister of the gospel. I said yes to God, and I can hardly believe what God has done through these years." In reality my dad never heard any voice. God spoke to him through a consecrated Sunday School teacher named Grace Featherstone. She has long since died and been forgotten. Sometimes the voice of God is heard through other people.

Usually Through Circumstances

Usually the voice of God is heard through our circumstances. Look up Acts 21:27. It doesn't really say much in itself that is of interest, but if you know the book of Acts, you are aware of the fact that in the life of the apostle Paul, this is a decisive turning point in the way God led Paul. Up until that time God led Paul in many different ways through people, visions, dreams, etc. But at that point, through the remaining chapters of Acts, every move Paul made was a result of circumstances in which God put him. He became a prisoner in Jerusalem, and he was never released again, as far as we know. Paul moved from Jerusalem to a ship. He did not decide to get on that ship. He was a prisoner and the Roman government moved him. God used him on the ship. There was a wreck. Paul was cast off on a little island. Paul did not pray about going to that island. He never saw a sign that directed him to the island. God sent a storm that washed him on the shores. Circumstances put him there; he couldn't help it. Paul moved from that island back to another ship and eventually to Rome. Every time he moved, right through until the end of his life, the government moved him. God saw to it that the government and Paul's circumstances put him exactly where He wanted him to be.

You will find that if you are right with God, if you are reading the Word of God, if you are in close fellowship with God, in most cases God will lead you, as He led the apostle Paul during the latter chapters of Acts, through the circumstances into which He places you.

It is very, very important in your life as a Christian to learn the secret of open and closed doors. If you are living for God, God will open the door through which He wants you to go, and God will close the door through which He does not want you to go.

You say, "Mr. Smith, sometimes there are two open doors, three open doors, or five open doors. For instance, right now I could go to Africa, I could go to Japan or I could go to South America. I have three possibilities. There are three different schools I might attend. There are five different jobs I might take. How do I know which of the open doors is the right door?"

I may say something that may disturb your ideas about God's leadership. However, the longer I live the more I am convinced that the will of God has a great deal more to do with our spiritual condition than it has with geographical location. I believe that if we are in the right place, in the right spiritual condition, we can take any one of the five doors and it will be right. If our spiritual condition is right, then we can move through any door that God opens and we will discover that God will use us there for His glory.

You say, "But what if I make a mistake?" Again, if your spiritual condition is right, God will turn you in another direction long before you make any serious mistake. But it has to do with your personal relationship with God. It is not as important that you know whether it is Africa or Japan, as it is that you know that you are right with God. The important question is not where should a man go, but rather what kind of man should go. Emphasize the *what,* not the *where* — spiritual condition, not geographical location.

Always — Through the Bible

Now you say, "Mr. Smith, this has been interesting, but I've never heard the voice of God audibly, I've never heard the voice of God through signs or other people, and if I were to take your advice and start going through open doors, I'm afraid I'd get terribly mixed up. How then can I hear the voice of God?"

May I suggest that, if you wish, you can forget each of these four points, if you'll remember this last one. Always the voice of God can be heard through His Word. This is the authoritative, infallible voice of God for you and for me now.

Sometimes I get a little tired of the people who are looking for the signs and the prophets and the visions and the dreams and all the rest of the dramatic things, when in their hands they hold God's Word. You say, "I don't know what God wants me to do." Isn't that strange, because I do. I've never seen most of you before, but I know what God is saying to you. He's saying many things, but let me leave you with just one. God is saying, "After that the Holy Ghost is come upon you, ye shall be witnesses unto me both in Jerusalem, and in all Judea, and in Samaria, and unto the uttermost part of the earth" (Acts 1:8). Just as surely as if God Almightly were standing here in the person of His Son on this Thursday evening of Founder's Week, God's voice is saying to every man and every woman and every boy and every girl in the building, "I want you to be a witness unto Me where you are and around the world."

While some of us are waiting to have some fantastic vision, dream, impression or sermon, we haven't yet responded to God's call to be a witness. That is God's voice. And unless a great many more of us hear it, respond to it, and do what He says, we will fail in our generation to get the gospel out to the ends of the earth.

God may speak audibly, through signs, through people, through circumstances, but always through the Word of God.

15

God's Four Calls

This sermon was also preached during Founder's Week at the Moody Bible Institute. However, it was three years earlier, February 6, 1964. It too, reflects my preaching rather than my writing.

****

I would like you to turn with me in your Bibles to the call of the apostle Paul to a specific country in the world. I think most people consider Paul the greatest missionary who ever lived, and this is the story of the day he received his specific missionary call and answered it.

"And a vision appeared to Paul in the night; There stood a man of Macedonia, and prayed him, saying, Come over into Macedonia, and help us. And after he had seen the vision, immediately we endeavoured to go into Macedonia, assuredly gathering that the Lord had called us for to preach the gospel unto them. Therefore loosing from Troas we came with a straight course to Samothracia, and the next day to Neapolis; and from thence to Philippi, which is the chief city of that part of Macedonia, and a colony: and we were in that city abiding certain days" (Acts 16:9-12).

There is a man in our church in Toronto who felt led to give twenty percent of his entire income to the Lord's work. We had a young man in our church by the name of Herb, who when he was about twenty-five years of age heard the call of God and felt that God had called him to spend his life in the mountains and in the jungles of Mexico, and he has done that. We have a woman in our church whom God called to spend her life being a mother, and she has done that and done it admirably, rearing five children, four boys and one girl. That's a bigger job than most missionaries do. We had a boy in our church by the name of David. When he was seventeen years of age God called him to man a hospital in the jungles of Ecuador. He has been doing that now for a number of years. We had another young man in our church named Bruce.

God called him into the ministry, and today Dr. Bruce Dunn pastors one of the great Presbyterian churches of America. I could go on down the list, as could any pastor.

If you were to sit across from these people whom I have mentioned and they were to tell you the story of their spiritual experience, I know them well enough to know what they would say without exception. The businessman I mentioned would say, "There was a day in my life when God called me to give twenty percent of my income, and I responded to that call." The man who spent his life in Mexico would say, "There was a day when I felt that God was calling me specifically to the country of Mexico, and I went." The woman who has reared four boys and one girl would perhaps sit back in her rocking chair today with a smile and say, "There was a time when God spoke to my heart and laid upon me the urgency of rearing a Christian family and I did it." The boy who has given his life in the jungles of Ecuador in that hospital removed from civilization would say, "There was a time when God laid the country of Ecuador before me. I felt that He wanted me to minister there, and I went." Dr. Bruce Dunn would tell you that there was a time when God called him to preach in the Grace Presbyterian Church of Peoria, Illinois. He responded to that call, and God has blessed his ministry in an abundant manner.

We have read from the Word of God the account of one of the first missionaries who received a call to a specific country, and you and I are Christians tonight because Paul received that call and answered it. However, if you will read your Bible you will discover that before the apostle Paul received the call to a specific country, he received three other calls from God. There are young people here who have been saying, "This is the thing I want to know; this is the burden of my heart; this is the thing I'm waiting for God to do. In some conference, or in some prayer meeting, or in some church, or on some lonely road I want to receive my call to a specific country. I would like to be able to say I know assuredly that this is what God wants me to do; this is where God wants me to go; this is the life God wants me to live. Then I would go ahead and do it. But I'm uncertain, I'm not quite sure. If somehow tonight God could pinpoint the country to which I am to go, I would rejoice that I had been at this service."

Before God calls you to your country, whether your country be a business office or a home or a hospital or a farm or a jungle or a riverbank or a pulpit, God will give you three other calls which you must answer first. The reason a great many people have never found their country is that they have never answered God's first three calls.

To Christ

Before God ever calls any person to a country, He calls him to Christ. You will find it in the Old Testament in words like these: "Come now, and let us reason together, saith the Lord: though your sins be as scarlet, they shall be as white as snow" (Isaiah 1:18). In the New Testament in the words of Jesus Christ, you find the call like this: "Come unto me, all ye that labour and are heavy laden, and I will give you rest" (Matt. 11:28). This is the call to Jesus Christ which goes out to every man, every woman, every boy, every girl, every place in this world. Until you hear and answer this call, you will never hear another call.

I think it is important to realize that the call to Christ is not a national affair. Sad to say we often associate religions with nations. When people say Japan, I automatically think of Buddhism. When people say North Africa, I immediately think of Mohammedanism. Sad to say, across this world, India reminds me of Hinduism; Irian Jaya of Animism, and so on. When the name of my country is used, or the name of your country is used most of the world immediately say, Christian. America, Canada, Great Britain, Australia, New Zealand, South Africa, Western Europe and others are the nominally Christian countries of the world, and there are a great many people who have so united these countries with the call of Christ that to them they are synonymous. I regret with most Americans the decision of the Supreme Court that bans prayer in schools. But one of its great advantages is this, it has pinpointed the fact that the word American and the word Christian are not synonymous terms.

The call to Christ is not a family call. I was reared in a pastor's home. I think one of the greatest heritages any boy or girl can have is the heritage of a godly father and a godly mother and the environment of a Christian home. But I know from my own experience that from the spiritual standpoint, being reared in a Christian home and associating in a Christian church can be a great spiritual embarrassment. I can still remember when I was a boy, I'd listen to an evangelist preach and my heart would be stirred and I would be convicted of my sin. There was a hunger in my soul, a need in my heart, a burden on my life. But as others raised their hands or walked down the aisle I would say, "I can't go. Why, if I walked down that aisle I'd embarrass my father to tears. Everybody in this building knows I'm a Christian, that I'm right with God. What would poor mother say if she saw her supposedly Christian son professing to the world that he really isn't a Christian?" For a long time I stood back where a great many pastors' sons have stood and where a great many sons and daughters of Christian parents stand or sit every Sunday night, watching others but embarrassed by a Christian family from doing it themselves.

As I stand in my pulpit every Sunday night I'm concerned about the strangers, but more than that, I'm concerned about our own boys and girls who sit there. I know many of them are not saved. They look saved, they act saved, and they have a saved facade. But I know from my own experience there are boys and girls who go to Sunday school every Sunday, take part in all the activities, wouldn't miss a Sunday night service for anything in the world; but they have never responded to the call to Jesus Christ and they are lost in the midst of a Christian environment. No wonder God doesn't call them to the mission field.

To Consecration

If you are ever going to get to that country after you have responded to the call of Jesus Christ, you will hear God's call to consecration. This comes to everybody who has responded to the call to Christ. You can find it in a great many places in the Bible, but perhaps one of the best verses is in the book of Romans. "I beseech you therefore, brethren, by the mercies of God, that ye present your bodies a living sacrifice, holy, acceptable unto God, which is your reasonable service" (Romans 12:1). No matter what else you may feel led to do, this call to consecration comes to every man, every woman, every boy and every girl everywhere in the world who has responded to the call of Christ.

One of the best ways to describe consecration is to think of your life as a house and to think of you as the owner of the house. You have a ring of keys. When you respond to the call to Christ you give God the front door key of your house, you commit your life to Jesus Christ. You say, "Here, take my life. I accept Jesus

Christ as my Saviour, I respond to the call to Christ." When you respond to the call to consecration, very methodically you take off the other keys from the ring and you give them to God one at a time.

For a mother or a father, consecration means that some day you enter the nursery in your home where lies the treasure of your heart and your life, and you walk up to that little bed where he sleeps, maybe a year, two years, three years, four years of age. You put your hands on the railing of that bed and you look up to God. You say, "Father in heaven, here is the key to the nursery. You gave me this child, you enabled me to bring him into the world. As long as you leave him with me, I'll look after him; I'll feed him, I'll love him, I'll clothe him, I'll guide him, I'll do everything I can for him, I'll give my life for him if necessary. But, Lord, this baby is yours, and if some day you want to take him out of my arms and put him in a jungle on the other side of the world where I know I'll never see him again, that's all right: He's yours. Or, Lord, if you just want to leave him here for four or five years and then take him back, he's yours. Lord, here is the key to the nursery."

This is consecration. Consecration is not something you do at the altar of the church; consecration is something you do on the roadway of life. Consecration is not something you do on your knees in a prayer room; consecration is something you do where you live. Consecration involves taking those things that are nearest and dearest to you and saying, "Lord God, they're not mine, they're yours."

For the young person, consecration means that he gives God the key to his education. Do you realize there are a great many young people who go through the years of their education as though it was theirs. They choose their schools as though it was their business. They do their studying as though they were the only ones concerned. They choose their courses for themselves. If you asked, they would say, "I'm a Christian, and as far as I know I'm dedicated. Why, I'm going to Bible school, or college. I'm headed for the ministry." Yet there has never really been a time in their lives when they have taken the key to their educational life and said, "Lord, this belongs to you. Every page I study I'm conscious that you are looking over my shoulder. Every examination for which I prepare is your business. Whether I succeed or whether I fail is your concern. The courses I take, the school I attend, the degree of attention with which I listen is your business, because you have the key to my educational life."

For the businessman, consecration means that there comes a day when he gives God the key to his business. This involves two things. It means the business has to be the kind that He can take over. And then it means it must be operated in a manner in which God can look over his shoulder and be pleased when He sees the books. This is consecration.

Then for all of us — and most of us will not like this very much — consecration means there is a time in our lives when we give God the key to our bank account. You say, "Mr. Smith, I can sit back and relax. I've been a tither for the last twenty years. I give God ten percent of everything I have and it has been the greatest blessing of my life." Yes, there is a great blessing in being a tither. But have you ever read this verse accurately? "I beseech you therefore, brethren, by the mercies of God, that from now on you give Almighty God ten percent of everything you have. This is what God expects you to do." That is what the Bible of ninety percent of Christians who tithe is supposed to say — but it doesn't.

I believe in tithing, and many people tithe, but I've never yet been able to preach a sermon on tithing from the New Testament. It's a good, solid Old Testament principle and it stops there. The New Testament principle is entirely different. Here is what it says: "I beseech you therefore, brethren, by the mercies of God, that you present your bodies" — this machine that God has given you with which you make every dollar you receive. God says He wants the entire machine, not just ten percent of the proceeds. There are a great many Christians who feel that they have written off their obligation to God when they have written a check and signed their name at the bottom of a tithe, but He should also own everything else I have. He should own every dollar I possess, every suit, every car, every house, every newspaper I buy. If there has been a time when Paul Smith has dedicated his life to God, then Paul Smith and everything Paul Smith has and everything he ever will have, already belongs to God.

That is what consecration is. There are some people waiting patiently for God to call them to a country, when all the time they have ignored God's call to consecration. They have never said, "Lord, here's the key ring. You can have access to every room in the house."

To College

Some of you will object to what I am about to say, but wait patiently if you will. First comes the call to Christ; that's for everybody. Secondly comes the call to consecration; that's for everybody who has responded to the call of Christ. Then comes the call to college.

I believe every consecrated Christian in the world should go to college. You say, "That's nonsense. Can't you see I'm a baldheaded man? Can't you see I'm all tied up in something else? I can't go to college." The sad part of our modern thinking is that we constantly try to pin God's call down to our unified standard of what is right. We establish the qualifications and then we expect God to call the people who have measured up to our educational standards. But God calls people — not always the ones who have taken the proper courses. There is a great difference. This is one thing I've always liked about the Bible colleges. For years they have been in the business of taking men and women whom they feel God has called, and starting with them there and trying to train them, instead of training them and then expecting God to call them after they have measured up to our standards — and remember they are *our* standards.

A little while ago a newspaper reporter in the city of Toronto said, "Mr. Smith, there is a great lack. Have you any suggestions that would give us more ministers and more missionaries?" The only thing I could think to say was this, "Remove any idea of a unified standard for service for God, and let men and women who are called by God get the best training they can from where they are." If God says yes, let us not say no because they don't meet our standards.

Having said that, let me say this: God expects everyone He is going to use to go to some kind of college, and there are a great many varieties. I think of Moses. Moses had possibly the longest college course on record. God wanted him to do a job. God knew exactly what He wanted him to do. But before he was ready to do it, God put him through a period of training that lasted forty years. After forty years of grooming, and training, and preparation, and spiritual enrichment, and humbling, then Moses saw the burning bush and received the call of God to a specific task; but not until he had gone to college.

The apostle Paul had the same experience, and incidentally, he was an educated man. Paul was saved on the Damascus Road, and if ever there was a man in the world who had a great testimony to give right then, he was that man. If I had been pastor of The Peoples Church in Jerusalem when Paul was saved, I'd have flown him into town the next Sunday night, and I would have kept him so busy from then on he wouldn't have had time to read a page of a book. But you see God has a great deal more sense than I have. God said, "No, Paul, you are not ready. Certainly I've done a great thing for you. Certainly you have a great testimony. But I can't use a man until he has been trained in some way."

For three years Paul studied under the training of the Lord Jesus Christ in Arabia. He was groomed and taught and ministered unto and prepared. In spite of the fact that during those three years millions of souls were dying, God took time to train him. After his training, after his grooming, after his preparation, then came the call from Macedonia, but not before.

These two men attended two absolutely different kinds of colleges, both men, greatly used of God, were trained before God could use them. There isn't an individual in the church who cannot be trained today. But how difficult it is to get the people of our churches to realize that to do a job for God they *need* to be trained. Almost every large church conducts a wonderful series of teacher training courses, but they are fortunate if they can get a corporal's guard to attend them. Yet every Sunday there are teachers who go before their Sunday School classes with the lives of boys and girls in their hands and the Word of God to be accurately dispensed, and all the while they have ignored a place where they could have been trained and groomed and prepared so that they could do the job God wants them to do. I believe this is one reason some of our young people throw their church overboard just as soon as they have a chance. They have sat under such pitiful teaching for twelve or thirteen years, they can't stand any more, because God's people have refused to go to college, they've refused to take the teacher training course.

You say, "Ours is just a little church. We don't have an educational director and we don't have any teacher training course." Have you ever thought of the great books that are available to God's people today? The influence of literature can be profoundly greater than the influence of preaching — it lasts longer. But do you know I have Christians in my church that I don't believe have read a book in a whole year. What a tragedy! On the library shelves in our churches, in our homes, in our bookstores is the potential of a tremendous college course that better prepares men and women to serve God, and the average church member leaves it, ignores it, thinks he can do without. Then he sits back and says, "Why doesn't God ask me to do something?" It's because he is not ready to do anything. He's not groomed, he's not prepared, he's not trained.

God will never put you in your country until first of all you go to the college that is available to you. If my memory serves me correctly, two of the great pastors of this church never had the advantage of a formal college education, but they were trained men. They used the sources that were available to them to learn, then they in turn were able to teach others. Oh, there is a great variety of colleges, and it is necessary for every Christian to go to college.

The world goes to college. Some of you businessmen right now are struggling through some kind of course in your business. After being out of school for twenty-five years you know how difficult it is. But executives realize that their men need to be trained and retrained again and again and again — a continual grooming in order to be their best for the business.

For young people, this training usually means an actual college course. This fabulous continent has more Bible schools and colleges of a Christian nature than any other in the world. Within a stone's throw of almost every major city there is a place where young people can be trained. And a great many young people have never received a call to a country because they haven't yet responded to the call of God that comes to every consecrated Christian to go to college.

To Country

Then we come to the last call, and I don't need to say anything about this, because if you have answered the first three calls you will find that there is a specific country where God wants you.

In 1940, outside the city of London, England, there was a small airport, with one air force officer in charge of a group of men. One night sirens all over the city of London began to wail, and seven or eight million people headed for the underground shelters. As they went underground, across the English Channel could already be heard the rumbling, that threatening sound of the German Luftwaffe with their loads of destruction. As they came closer and closer and closer, the officer in charge of the airfield turned to a little handful of men and said, "You man the anti-aircraft guns." And they did it, but there weren't enough of them. He turned to another pitiful little handful of men and said, "You man the searchlights." And they did, but there were far too few. He turned to the smallest group of all and said, "You climb into the Hurricanes and the Spitfires and go up to meet the enemy." They did it, but there were so few it was almost funny.

But at that time perhaps somebody might have looked off toward the great city of London where there were three or four million men and might have said, "With all that manpower, why in the world didn't that air force officer point to ten thousand men and say, 'You get on the anti-aircraft guns'? Why didn't he turn to another ten thousand men and say, 'You man the searchlights'? Why didn't he turn to another twenty thousand and say, 'You fly up and wipe the enemy out of the sky'?"

I'll tell you why. Two or three years before that time a general call went out to all the young men of Great Britain, urging them to join the air force. A handful of men responded, and during those two or three years they were trained, they were prepared, they were groomed, they were disciplined; but twenty million men went on with their jobs. When the moment of truth came, the only people of any use to that commander was that handful of men who two or three years before had answered the general call to arms and now were ready to do a specific job.

Off in the distance in this old sin-cursed world it seems I can hear the rumble of the Luftwaffe of the devil. It's moving across our nations at an alarming rate. Already it has cast an enormous impregnable cloud across one-third of the world's population and removed them from our reach. As I look across the world, in Japan I see a little handful of missionaries, and I say, "There are far too few." I look down to South America where there are millions of people and I see another handful of missionaries and I say, "Far too few." I look across to Africa with its budding nations, and in that country which is one of the most heavily populated missionary countries in the world there are far too few. And so on around the world. The laborers are few.

Then I open up the statistics books of the evangelical churches of the Christian countries of the world, and what do I see? I see our Christian population numbered in terms of millions, and the question in my own heart is this: In this desperately needy world, with its pitiful conditions, in which men and women are going into a Christless eternity moment by moment, why doesn't the church of Jesus Christ bring together ten thousand missionaries and send them to the land of Japan and claim it for Jesus Christ? Why don't we get another ten thousand missionaries and put them into the countries of South America so that a person can't go ten miles without running into one? Why don't we find another ten thousand missionaries and send them into India and another ten thousand to the islands of the sea? We have the people, but do you know why we don't do it? They haven't answered the first three calls. Our people aren't ready.

Somewhere there is a country with your name on it. I don't know where it is. I don't know who lives there, but there are people there. They are alive now and God is waiting to say, "George, Betty, Bill, Jack, Bob, I want you over there." Maybe it will be a hospital, maybe it will be a store, maybe it will be a jungle, maybe it will be a riverboat, maybe it will be a pulpit, maybe it will be a home. Somewhere there's a country with your name on it, and the people are there waiting for you to come. But God can't send you until you have responded to the call to Christ, the call to consecration, and the call to college. Only then can you expect to hear the call of God to your country.

May God help us in this desperate world to be ready, and when the call comes to be able to say, "Assuredly this is of God," and set our course straight, so that our country will have our ministry in response to God's call.